the de-stress diva's guide to life

77 ways to recharge, refocus, and reorganize your life

WILEY
John Wiley & Sons, Inc.

contents

acknowledgments

I don't even know where to begin in thanking all the people who have made this book so special.

It all started with my agent, June Clark, who believed in me and this project from the start. I loved meeting you in New York, June.

I have thoroughly enjoyed working with my editor at Wiley, Christel Winkler, who really helped me keep the stress down while I was writing this book. I love your easygoing spirit, Christel.

I have so many Earth Angels who made this book possible by helping me keep on track. Just a few of them: my children, Naomi, David, and Daniel, who continually remind me how beautiful life can be; Judy and George Benz, who provide a home spa environment for my body, for my soul, and for my emotions; Renee Piane, who is the best love coach a friend can have; Melodee Hunt, my administrative assistant and friend, who always balances reality with love; Theresa Baisden, who checked in on me daily for months; my brother, Sherman Gross, whose warmth and strong sixth sense reminded me of my heritage; and Barbara Lincoln, whose words and wisdom helped me stay on a lit path. You are the ones who kept me going when times were rough, who kept me laughing when I didn't feel like laughing, and who believed in me when I was having doubts. To all of you, *thank you* for sharing your wisdom, your time, and your hearts.

To all my other Earth Angels, you are too numerous to list, but you know who you are and you know I keep you safely tucked away in my heart.

introduction

Think how much happier, healthier, and more fulfilled we would be if each of us had our own de-stress kit to minimize the stress of daily living.

Inside this book, you'll find myriad ways to downshift the stress in your life. You will find simple tips to help you avoid stress when you can, and better weather it when you cannot.

As I was completing the book, I received a call from Cynthia, a dear friend with whom I had not spoken in a long time. She left a message saying that she had been diagnosed with breast cancer and was recalling the people in her life who made her laugh and inspired her; the real gift was that I was one of them. Cynthia and I began to socialize again on a regular basis. As divine serendipity enjoys the dance of life, so too, did we enjoy our conversations about stress and cancer. Through her cancer treatment, Cynthia learned a lot about herself and noticed some of the red flags surrounding her lifestyle choices. She had not seen them when she was in the midst of living her busy lifestyle. I asked Cynthia what her points of stress overload had been. She told me they were exhaustion, lack of mental clarity, and lack of physical strength. She said, "Recognizing that I stuffed my emotions, I stopped laughing."

1

She realized her life was out of balance; it was mostly work, with a little family time and a little time with her friends. She did not exercise or watch what she ate.

When you read this book, I urge you to use the de-stress tips while following the guidance from your heart. This will allow you to remain mindful of what you're doing and focused on the present moment. Cynthia shared with me that she never noticed or appreciated many things in her life. She was living from her intellect rather than her heart.

Stress does not discriminate between the poor or rich, women or men, younger people or older people. Through my work with clients ranging from teenagers to stay-at-home parents, and from solo entrepreneurs to Fortune 500 captains of industry, I know that unbridled stress can wreak havoc on anyone's work, health, relationships, goals, and dreams. Our thoughts, positive or negative, are the foundation for who and what we become in our lives and in our relationships.

I have lived a full life replete with my own share of stress and emotional pain. The daughter of two Holocaust survivors, I have raised my own children through the highs and lows of modern life and relationship losses. Through my personal experiences, I have accumulated many ideas that help downshift the stress in life and to find the joy again, not just for my clients but for myself.

As you read this book, I urge you to be kind to yourself, and honor the person you truly are inside. It is possible to be calm and not give in to negative stress, even in the face of terrible crises. It is also possible to learn, forget, and then re-learn how best to reduce your stress. My hope is this book becomes your lifelong guidebook.

I did not write this book because I never experience stress, and I certainly did not do it because I have mastered stress 100 percent of the time. On the contrary, I have experienced great amounts of stress and have searched for and found numerous ways to counteract it, and now I will share all my hard-won tips with you!

forget perfect

1 think positive

We can sabotage the positive ways in which we begin and end each day when we let negative thoughts gain control of our minds. Negatives attract negatives, and negative thinking can cause chronic, dangerously high levels of stress. To downshift the speed and the stress in our lives, we must ratchet down our tendencies to expect the worst or beat ourselves up for things we did or didn't do.

The ordinary stress in our daily lives can be exacerbated by negative thinking and can lead to high levels of hostility, according to a study published by the *Journal of Psychosomatic Medicine*. Positive thinking, on the other hand, can benefit our physical health, reported researchers at the University of Wisconsin–Madison. The study suggests that people with positive attitudes have less risk of developing heart disease and have lower levels of stress hormones.

dear diva

"I often obsess about situations I find stressful, and I'm exhausted and tense so much of the time. How can I make healthy changes?"

secrets from the de-stress diva

Our thoughts color our perceptions and our experiences in life. If there is one thing that we can focus on 99 percent of the time, it is our thoughts. If we are able to focus, we will readily "see" the hundreds of thoughts that arise each day. Here is a simple, yet insightful, way to become aware of your thoughts. It will help you understand your behavior, increase your energy level, and improve your ability to enjoy relationships.

Thought Exercise

Carry around a notepad and write down your thoughts every fifteen to thirty minutes for two full days, from the moment you wake up until just before you fall asleep. You will be amazed at what comes up. Once you identify where your thoughts take you and how they dictate your feelings toward yourself and others, you will have a perfect place to start making changes. Don't be like most people and try to change your thinking process without understanding your own thought patterns.

Here are a few examples of how different individuals express their thought patterns:

The "Yes, but" pattern. This response comes from people who "listen" to what you're saying but, more often than not, will insert a "yes, but" reason why they can't do something.

The "Maybe, we'll see" pattern. People who find it difficult to make a decision react in this way. Perhaps they are afraid to make "wrong" decisions, and thus choose not to decide or to delay their answers.

The "Sitting on the fence" pattern. This pattern of thinking may be the result of people not taking the time to sit quietly and get in touch with themselves. Once individuals can identify and understand their values, they can analyze the pros and cons of every action or decision. Then they can assess how the ramifications of each choice would measure up to their core values. Suddenly, they will know the right answer.

The "That won't work because" pattern. People with this pattern think that if they or other people have previously tried and failed at something, there is no reason why it would work this time. They don't realize that some ideas are too advanced for their time, or that a person's thoughts and confidence level or even a slight change in implementation may bring about a positive outcome.

The "Everything is a drama" pattern. Certain people complain about all the drama, even though drama is what they bring to every task. They will become tired of the drama only when they stop playing dramatic characters in their lives or with specific people or situations. Sometimes we think that being involved in a drama is the only "safe" way to express our emotions, even if these have nothing to do with the situation at hand.

Our thoughts create our world: our lives, our relationships with ourselves and with others. Be the positive change you want to see in your life. An optimistic and calm spirit will shine brightly from within a person, as well as outward to others. We each have the ability to bring sunshine and positive energy to the world.

Meditation

One of the fastest ways to get rid of, or at least minimize, obsessive thoughts or "stuck" thinking patterns is to meditate. Once you have been consistently meditating a little each day for a week, you will be able to create a quiet space in your mind within a minute or less. Remember to be kind to yourself and to honor your thoughts, but don't get downhearted or depressed by them.

Here's a quick, easy meditative technique:

1. Sit up straight in a chair or on the floor.
2. Close your eyes and be mindful of your breathing: breathing in . . . breathing out.
3. When good or bad thoughts come up, simply thank them for appearing and let them go for now.
4. Return to your focus on breathing.

This meditative state will help you to *stop* your obsessive thoughts, long enough to get a grip on your emotions or perhaps a new perspective on the situation.

Aromatherapy

1. When you feel your thoughts taking over and you lack focus, write down the thoughts that are preventing you from moving forward. Just get them out of your head by writing them down.
2. Use this lotion formula to massage into your hands:
   - Add six drops sandalwood essential oil to four teaspoons olive oil.
   - Rub a few drops of this mixture into your hands, up to your forearms.
   - Now breathe in and focus on moving forward with inspiration.

3. Think of a positive statement or mantra and repeat it to yourself until you feel the focus and the motivation to move forward.

Gratitude

One universal law says, "That which we focus on and give attention to appears." You may want to share a gratitude statement that I often use: "I appreciate the beauty all around me and am grateful for what I *do* have."

Food

Artichokes contain high levels of B vitamins, and these vitamins help to increase our energy and mental alertness. Both qualities are necessary for us to maintain a cheerful, optimistic attitude.

Recent research suggests that inflammation is the origin of all degenerative diseases, such as heart disease, arthritis, Alzheimer's, Parkinson's, and so forth. Nature's inflammation fighters come in the guise of fruits. Papayas, pineapples, and kiwifruit contain large amounts of the anti-inflammatory enzyme bromelain, which can lessen the inflammatory process.

> daily aspiration   "I love and accept myself just the way I am."

2 do you see the glass as half-full or half-empty?

The Wharton School of Business reports that a positive attitude can increase productivity on the job and can inspire more congenial responses from managers and coworkers. "Feelings drive performance," the research study concluded.

dear diva

"My thoughts sometimes make me so nervous and irritable. How can I avoid being so anxious and over the top?"

secrets from the de-stress diva

I often say it's all in the attitude. I founded the Self-Esteem Council with four other incredible women, and we work with high school students. One course in our five-month program teaches students that it's not so much what happens to us, but how we handle what comes our way. We all know of people who have beaten the odds in a number of situations. In fact, some of our favorite inspirational movies are in this category: *Rudy, Erin Brockovich, Stand by Me.* (By the way, all of these films are based on real-life stories.)

My dad once told me that his mom never minded making the beds of her nine children. Why? Because she was so grateful that they were not in them, which meant that her children were healthy and either in school or playing. I often remembered that "attitude of gratitude" in relation to my own three children, when their bedrooms appeared as if a hurricane, a whirlwind, and an earthquake had all hit at once. I merely shut the door and said to myself, Thank you, God . . . they're healthy.

Attitudes of Gratitude

Here are some other attitudes of gratitude I often keep in mind. I'm grateful for:

- Hearing my friends or family members answer the phone because I know they are still alive.
- The chore of washing and blow-drying my hair because I'm fortunate to have hair.
- Listening to the birds sing early in the morning because I know that my hearing is still sharp.
- Spending the money to fill up my gas tank because I have a safe car to drive.
- Sneezing when I'm near dust because I know that my immune system is doing its job.

- Having too much to do on some days because I know that my life is not boring.
- Not understanding new software programs because it gives my brain a run for its money and allows me to stay alert and agile, while always learning something new.

Let It Go

Every time you feel stressed or overwhelmed, write down your thoughts at that moment. Look at them and then *let them go*! Watch the thoughts leave your mind as if whisked away to the heavens by a breeze. Now, focus on calm and positive thoughts. You are laying the groundwork to establish a positive attitude.

Breathe

Take in a deep breath and then exhale. With your outward breath, visualize and feel your negative thoughts, angry emotions, resentment, and so on, flowing out. Then consciously breathe in peaceful words, such as *calm, loving,* and *safe*. Once you can truly feel this calm, loving space, then continue to breathe out the negative emotions or attitudes and breathe in the corresponding opposite emotions. In other words, you will breathe out anger and breathe in calmness; breathe out resentment and breathe in forgiveness; breathe out blame and breathe in personal responsibility; and so forth.

Sing

Select your theme song. Is there a song that makes you feel happier and more centered whenever you sing it? Years ago, my theme song was "I Am Woman." Today, my theme song is "Perfect Day" by Hoku.

Keep a song handy on your iPod, CD, or MP3 player that empowers you when you sing it at the top of your lungs.

Read Success Stories

A great way to keep your motivation up and your attitude positive is to read stories about successful people and businesses and how they may have gone bust one or more times before making it.

Decaf Your Coffee or Better Yet . . .

Even decaffeinated coffee has some caffeine in it. Plus, most coffees are decaffeinated through the use of methylene chloride, a chemical that interferes with the blood's ability to deliver oxygen. This obviously makes the heart work harder to supply oxygen to all of the cells. Make sure that the caffeine has been removed from your decaffeinated coffee with a water-processing method.

Or, you could switch to teas that are high in antioxidants, such as white, green, or roobius teas. Or, gradually change to a caffeine-free herbal coffee, Teeccino. I like the taste of Almond Amaretto, so I started with ¾ cup organic coffee and ¼ cup Almond Amaretto Teeccino; the second week I used ½ cup coffee and ½ cup Teeccino; the third week I used ¾ cup Teeccino and ¼ cup coffee; and by the fourth week I was drinking a full cup of Teeccino. I still use the same amount of soymilk that I would have with my regular organic coffee.

Royal Jelly

Royal jelly is known to enhance energy and immunity and is rich in vitamins and collagen. It's used to feed queen bees. When a queen bee is fed the same exact diet as the worker bees, the queen lives for only seven to eight weeks, the same life span as the worker bees. In the perfect balance of nature, queen bees are fed only royal jelly, and they live for five to seven years. Just make sure that you're not allergic to bee venom because you may also be sensitive to other substances made by bees.

daily aspiration   "I will keep my attitude and thoughts positive as I move through the day and encounter people, places, and things."

3 be careful of the superwoman urge

The book *The Superman Syndrome: Why the Information Age Threatens Your Future and What You Can Do about It*, by Robert Kamm, focuses on the dangers of thinking that today's 24/7 technology can make you turn into a 24/7 superhero. The book reports on studies showing that 70 percent of people who work in offices during the week also work on weekends.

dear diva

"There's so much I have to do that if *I* don't do it, I know it won't get done . . . or worse, won't get done properly."

secrets from the de-stress diva

What would *really* happen if you didn't do it all? Plus, why are *you* taking all the responsibility to do everything? I want you to first ask yourself, "What need am I fulfilling by being the Supermom or the Superdad?" Do you need to be seen, heard, or applauded? Do you need to be better than someone else, or do you feel that you're not good enough? (It's the same thing, really.)

Identify and understand why you need to go to extremes to be great in every area of your life. For Supermoms and Superdads, does that mean you have to take your children to every possible extracurricular activity and bake cookies afterward?

Make a List

Make a list with "Positive Energy" at the top of one column and "Draining Energy" at the top of another column. List all of the activities you perform, aligning them beneath the heading that categorizes them. If your answer is "I don't know," list that activity in the "Draining Energy" column.

Next comes the difficult part. I want you to stop doing one of the activities listed in the "Draining Energy" column. I don't care how you stop it, but stop doing it. This is where creativity comes in. In most cases, all you have to do is accept the fact that you are willing to let this activity go. When you do, an idea will spring up in your mind that gives you information or a choice, including the option to delegate the activity to someone else or to completely change course.

For example, one of my clients was a stay-at-home mom who enjoyed her four children and their activities very much. She found, however, that she was overcommitted with the children's activities. One day she was really strapped for time because she had to bake chocolate chip cookies for one of her children's classroom parties. I asked her what was it about the chocolate chip cookies that made her tense. She said that she just didn't have time to take the kids to school, do some errands, bake, and come back to the school. I asked her why she wanted to bake the cookies, and she said, "Because I always have." I asked whether her child or the kids in the classroom would care if the cookies were store-bought from a bakery or made from scratch. Her response: "I don't think they'll know any difference." When she heard herself say those words, the Supermom lightbulb switched on. As it turned out, she was baking the cookies to fit her idea of what a good mother did, not for the children's taste buds. She soon realized that what was really important was her attendance at the school party and her love for her child.

Ask yourself this question frequently as you go about your normal day: What responsibilities do I take on that prevent others from participating or taking personal responsibility for doing things themselves? The best way to help children and adults gain self-confidence is to allow them to personally take responsibility for doing things. That's a very healthy way to learn at any age.

Yoga

"Our nervous and endocrine systems can be thrown off by chronic stress. The more you can, keep your hormones stable," said Sierra Bender, the creator of the popular Boot Camp for Goddesses workshops. Yoga is one way to help restore balance to your body and promote vibrant health and sustained energy. Yoga exercises for beginners or for those with advanced skills can be found on the Internet, at local yoga classes, or in books at the library.

Nature

Go outside and focus on nature for five minutes. Notice how the trees, the leaves, the branches, the birds, the sunlight, and the wind work in harmony without stress. So much of nature's beauty and peace comes from our mindfully "seeing" how nature is in harmony with its surroundings, even with man-made homes, buildings, roads, or walls in the vicinity.

Aromatherapy

1. Add four drops of lavender essential oil to eight table-spoons of water and pour this mixture into a spray bottle.
2. Close your eyes, take a deep breath, and think of a calming word. As you breathe out, mist your face.
3. Keep breathing with your eyes shut, and spend a few minutes focusing on what you need to do. Prioritize your schedule, while being mindful not to overdo it. Don't be a Supermom. Downshift into a more fulfilling, less stressful role, and the people around you will notice and appreciate it.

> daily aspiration "I love and accept myself just the way I am."

4 has your stress thermostat reached "overwhelmed"?

Often, the feeling of being overwhelmed will stifle our actions and thoughts and prevent us from moving forward. Most people who feel overwhelmed spend a great deal of time spinning their wheels as they overthink their situation, or they feel guilty for not making progress in their lives. A major symptom of feeling overwhelmed is procrastination. I don't believe that procrastinators are lazy. Rather, I think that they just have so much to do, they don't know where to start. Or perhaps they want to start, but they don't really know what to do or how to do it.

A study by the nonprofit Families and Work Institute reported that one in three U.S. employees is chronically overworked, and that more than half feel overwhelmed at least once a month. The study also found that 21 percent of those who are overwhelmed experience symptoms of clinical depression—more than twice the rate of employees who are not overworked.

dear diva

"I have too much to do and feel overwhelmed and out of control. How can I manage my time better?"

secrets from the de-stress diva

When you feel overwhelmed, this is what I want you to do:

1. Write down all the things that make you feel overwhelmed, including relationships, tasks, calls, e-mail, filing, and so forth.

2. Choose the top ten things that are essential for you to do.

3. Choose only two items to begin or to complete before you move on to any of the other items. Then, choose two calls, two e-mails, and so on—two things from each category. I call this the Rule of Two. To choose the two items, decide which two items need to be

done so that if you don't do anything else that day, you will still feel as if you accomplished something important. Notice that I didn't say that you will feel as if you accomplished *something*, because just having lunch means that you accomplished eating. So, please be sure that the two items (and calls, e-mails, and errands) you choose are important.

Breathe

Our emotions are directly connected to our breathing. When we're nervous or fearful, our breathing is usually shallow. So, one of the best places to start when you feel overwhelmed is to take in a slow and deep breath, hold it a few seconds, and then slowly exhale. You may want to do this two or three times to fully calm your mind and get oxygen circulating in your brain to boost creativity and mental power.

Yoga

You can do the following exercise at home or in the office.

1. Sit down comfortably in a chair, with your feet squarely on the floor.
2. Breathe in deeply as you slowly raise your arms above your head, palms facing forward. Breathe out while keeping your arms straight and lower them in front of you, along with your upper torso, as if bowing. Gently stretch so that your head is down between your knees and your arms are hanging in front of your legs. Be sure to keep breathing.
3. Slowly start to sit up, one vertebra at a time, so that you don't hurt your back or become dizzy.

Nutritional Solution

Strawberries are rich in B vitamins, vitamin C, flavonoids, and fiber so they're heart healthy and good for digestion. They also help to destroy environmental toxins and alleviate stress-related conditions.

You may even want to grab a glass of fresh veggie juice when you feel stressed and overwhelmed and your anxiety is over the top. Combine the following ingredients in a blender:

A large handful of kale
A large handful of spinach
A little fresh ginger
1 carrot
1 apple

Energy Drainers

We often go through our days without realizing that we are losing energy. Many unsettling thoughts and problems swirl through our minds: that recent miscommunication with a coworker, feeling deluged with requests and demands on our time, the annoyance of sitting in traffic when we're in a hurry, or myriad other anxiety-producing experiences in modern life.

I want you to focus on what brings you joy and what brings you down. In other words, first think of the people, the things, the activities, and the places that make you happy and add to your energy. Then mentally list the people, the things, the activities, and the places that bring you down, drain your energy, and zap your body of vitamins and minerals.

Did you know that when you feel stressed, the vitamin balance in your body can be disrupted, and you end up with a vitamin, mineral, and/or amino acid imbalance? These imbalances then cause "dis-ease," said Dr. John Neustadt, a naturopathic doctor.

Keep track of the people, activities, and things that give you a boost or that drain your energy for a week. You'll be amazed at what you discover. Be mindful of how you're feeling and of the amount of stress you experience, rating it from 1 to 10 (10 being your highest stress level). You will find a Stress Sheet to use for this exercise at my Web site, www.destressdiva.com/energy. After you have filled it in for a week, review it to find patterns.

Dance

Play some of your favorite high-powered music and start dancing. You may want to put on a song with a slower rhythm for gentle dancing. The most important thing is that you dance to your heart's desire and keep your movements free flowing.

> daily aspiration "Today I take one thing at a time."

5 time to focus on what is most important … now

Setting priorities is crucial to achieving our goals for each day and for our lives, yet our personal priorities often become lost because of our hectic schedules.

A report from the Mayo Clinic cites several modern factors that disrupt our efforts to establish priorities. Our global economy has created a round-the-clock mind-set in how we view work, which also affects the hours we set aside for our personal lives and priorities.

Advanced communication technologies have led to a loss of personal down time; we are always "on" or accessible. These technologies also distract our attention from the here and now—activities we may be absorbed in or people we are interacting with. Today's families, in which two or more members may be fully immersed in the world of work, must struggle to maintain quality relationships within the family unit and with friends.

dear diva

"How do I rise above the distractions, focus on the most important priorities, and achieve real results?"

secrets from the de-stress diva

Not setting priorities is one of the main reasons that people feel stressed and overwhelmed. Setting priorities stems from being very clear about your values. If you have identified your five most important values, then setting priorities becomes so much easier. For example, my top five priorities are God, family, work, exercise, and play. So, if there is a meeting in the evening and one of my children asks me out to dinner, I will almost always choose spending time with my family. Why? My family is a higher priority than my work, even though my work is very important to me.

What are your top three highest values? What are the top three highest priorities in your life, in general?

Now I want you to make a "worry" list:

1. Write down all of your worries and/or all the things that make you feel overloaded and stressed out.

2. Look at this list closely and categorize the worries into personal, home, specific person, work, organization, and so forth.

3. Now decide which items on this "worry" list are causing you stress because of your feelings and reactions or because of time pressures.

4. Which tasks can you delegate to someone else?

5. How can you "reframe" your stress or worried feelings and reactions to calm yourself down and see the situation more positively?

6. Now consider how this new reframing and the projects you have delegated allow you to focus on your priorities. Do you have more quality time and a better outlook as a result?

Thoughts

Shut your eyes and imagine that you do not have the gift of sight for two minutes. Slowly open your eyes and "see" how you feel now.

Breathe

Sit quietly and breathe in a slow, relaxed manner. Lovingly let your feelings of being stressed or worried arise, and then "thank" them as you let them go. Feelings are not facts; they are information. Our feelings are trying to tell us something, and we need to pay attention to the information, not dwell on the stress and the pain.

Now that you have let your stress and obsessive thoughts go, tell yourself, "I have enough time to accomplish my top priorities right now."

Take a Walk

Take a walk for about five or ten minutes and be mindful only of the scenery while you are walking. Leave your anxious thoughts and stress behind. If they crop up in your mind, simply be kind to yourself and say, "Thank you" and "Good-bye." Or loudly tell yourself to "Stop!"

Aromatherapy

If you feel that you need to refocus and lift your spirits and emotions so that you can focus on your priorities, you may want to use essential oils that stimulate the mind, such as peppermint, various citruses, and even basil. Terri Hicks, an aromatherapist, said, "These are excellent uplifters."

Acupressure

Eastern societies believe that healthy chi, or the flow of energy through the body, is important in order to maintain your vigor and well-being.

By pressing areas on your face and head, you can stimulate chi and, as a result, release tension.

1. Using your index finger, quickly and gently tap various spots on your face.
2. Using the fingertips of both hands, rhythmically and gently tap the sides of your head a few times.

Food

Astragalus is known to increase vitality and prevent colds and flu. It has been used in Asia for more than two thousand years and is considered an excellent antiaging herb. Astragalus also helps heal skin wounds and infections.

> daily aspiration   "I am calm and peaceful and I feel inner joy."

6 uncork your feelings

There's science to back up the long-held advice that sharing your feelings can help you to alleviate stress. A 2007 brain-imaging study by UCLA psychologists found that the simple act of verbalizing feelings elicits useful insights or advice from the listener. The study also found that expressing your feelings in writing, such as by keeping a journal, is beneficial in reducing stress.

dear diva

"I get so angry sometimes, I wish I could just express my feelings out loud. But I'm afraid I'll be judged as weak or whining. Instead, I bottle everything up and just want to scream by the end of the week. How can I express my feelings?"

secrets from the de-stress diva

We are full of emotions, and it is important to frequently "empty out" our feelings and emotions. Putting them in writing is a healthy way to do this. It allows us to gain perspective on what we feel and, as a result, lowers our stress levels.

1. **Keep a journal.** People are often afraid to express their feelings because they fear that these will be misinterpreted. Express your feelings on paper, to yourself, first. Keep a journal and write down what you feel when a stressful situation arises. Keeping a journal is an enlightened way to explore your stress-triggers, as you track what makes you feel stressed and why.

2. **Use your journal as your script.** Revisit what you have written in your journal to avoid blurting out your feelings to others first. When you have had a chance to dispassionately examine your feelings on paper, you will be calm and thoughtful (versus angry or overemotional) when you express your feelings to others.

3. **Find a trusted sounding board.** Ask a friend to become your sounding board, in exchange for your being that person's sounding board. Promise each other that you won't pass judgment or even offer advice but will only listen. In Great Britain, there are social organizations that offer professional "listeners" to workplaces, not

to offer advice, but merely to act as sounding boards. If you're hesitant to express your feelings to a boss or a family member, practice with your trusted sounding board first.

What Is Your Emotional Temperature?

In the wonderful play *Wicked*, a prequel to the children's classic *The Wizard of Oz*, the characters don't say, "Wait a minute." They say, "Just wait a tick-tock!" At home and at work, we tend to be obsessed with watching the tick-tock of the clock. But before we resort to the same old habit, we can tackle our emotions, which so often control how we measure time. We all have what I call an "emotional thermostat," and we each have a different emotional boiling point. Just as water boils at 212 degrees Fahrenheit, we, too, have a temperature at which our emotions boil. Once we hit that boiling point, our creativity fizzles and our body goes into fight-or-flight mode. We've all experienced this when our stress is in overdrive and perhaps we have just had an altercation with a colleague or a family member. As we walk away from that person, we think of all the things we could have said but didn't think of. That is exactly what happens: our fight-or-flight response overrides our creative thinking.

Emotions Feed Our Energies

Turning a negative emotion (the feeling of being overwhelmed, fearful, or anxious or just being in a bad mood) into a positive one can reenergize us.

A study conducted by the Wharton School of Business at the University of Pennsylvania reports that "positive people cognitively process more efficiently and more appropriately." People in a negative mood tend to inefficiently spend too much processing time on the mood itself. The Wharton research report found that when in a positive mood, people are more open to taking in information and handling it effectively. Here are two de-stress strategies you can use:

1. **Make a choice.** The choice to approach your day in a negative way or a positive way is entirely up to you. Instead of allowing yourself to feel overwhelmed, take positive action

by breaking up your many tasks for the day into only two to do at a time. Concentrate on one page at a time in order to finish a report. Go room by room to clean your house or deal with home maintenance problems. Take one step at a time to reach your healthy eating or exercise goals. It's all up to you.

2. **Try it out.** Spend five minutes writing down your to-do list on a piece of paper. Circle the two most important items. Tackle those first. Then return to your list and repeat the exercise. It's hard to feel positive when you feel overwhelmed. It's easy to be positive when you know you can accomplish one thing first, then another, and then another.

Focus on Your Decisions Today for a Happier Tomorrow

It's hard to hear sometimes, but for the most part, our current lives consist of the decisions we have made along the way. Where we are today is a culmination of those decisions. Jack Canfield, the coauthor of the Chicken Soup for the Soul books and the author of *Success Principles*, says in the first chapter of *Success Principles* that we need to take 100 percent responsibility for our lives right now.

Become conscious of all your decisions. Look at the decisions you make daily, starting in the morning; for example, did you have breakfast? Did you exercise or did you feel there wasn't enough time? Did you stop for a moment and say something loving to your child or spouse before leaving for the day? Did you decide to work through lunch to meet a deadline or did you refuel your body and your mind by taking time off for lunch? Continue to be conscious of your decisions during the day for the next week. You may be motivated to make different types of decisions.

> daily aspiration   "I will honor my feelings today and then let them go."

7 expectations are a setup for frustration

Having high expectations of others can lead to self-imposed stress when people fail to meet your expectations. To reduce your stress levels, downgrade your expectations, not only of yourself but of others, too. One New Zealand study suggests that "putting things into perspective" can help diffuse stress that is caused by others failing to meet your expectations.

dear diva

"I work hard, but everything falls apart when other people fail to do their jobs, too. Their failures make me look like a failure. How can I avoid the frustration that always arises when I have to depend on others to get a job done?"

secrets from the de-stress diva

1. **Be realistic.** If you feel frustrated when people fail to perform at the level that your expectations have set for them, then lower the bar. Expecting what's impossible of others will only guarantee disappointment. Step back and ask yourself what you realistically can expect from your family members, friends, contractors, or employees. Then plan your tasks accordingly.

2. **Listen.** Oftentimes, in setting yourself up for failure by expecting too much of others, you fail to listen to other people. Instead of making demands, ask whether your request can be met. You might hear an answer that will allow you to better coordinate a partnership or a project without the stress that comes with "guessing" but not knowing whether an expectation can be met.

3. **Focus on your priorities.** If your personal priorities rely on whether others can meet your high expectations, then revisit your priorities. Focus your priorities on yourself, not on setting priorities for other people. If you keep your focus on your own goals, you won't overrely on others.

Are You Playing the Blame Game?

Sometimes we expect too much of others as an excuse to blame someone else for our own failures. Ask yourself, why are you demanding so much of someone else? Are you taking full responsibility for your actions, regardless of how the other person acts? This is an exercise best practiced in your personal journal, which will allow you to write down, examine, and then revisit your answers to learn whether you are guilty of playing the blame game.

Expect Good Food First

When people find that they have misinterpreted their expectations of one another, here's a good, nonthreatening way to determine whether a group is a "good fit" for a project or a partnership. Plan a meal in which your guests bring their talents to the table in the form of a dish. Plan a family meal or a work-focused picnic. Allow participants to volunteer their strengths in presenting certain dishes and to acknowledge their weaknesses in allowing someone with more skill to prepare other dishes. The give-and-take of the planning process, the execution, and the enjoyment of the meal can set the stage for more productive partnerships that acknowledge that everyone can share in getting a job done.

> daily aspiration   "I am confident of my own decisions and strengths."

8 laughter de-stresses the spirit

It seems that laughter really is the best medicine. Researchers at Loma Linda University in California report that laughing reduces stress hormones, lowers blood pressure, relaxes tense muscles (especially a good belly laugh), triggers the release of endorphins, and boosts immune functions. Best yet, it's free!

Researchers at the University of Maryland School of Medicine have linked laughter to the healthy functioning of our blood vessels, which can stave off heart disease. The researchers showed funny movies to their test subjects and discovered that people experienced an increase in blood flow throughout their bodies. Laughter apparently causes the tissue that forms the inner lining of our blood vessels, the endothelium, to contract and expand to increase the blood flow. Laugh out loud. It's good for your health, as well as for reducing your stress levels.

dear diva

"I don't have time to do my job, take care of my home, and meet every other overwhelming obligation in my week. How can I find more time to have fun?"

secrets from the de-stress diva

So, go ahead. Rent a funny movie. Visit a witty friend. Read a humorous book, it's good for you!

- **Rent a funny movie.** You can catch up on simple chores such as filing paperwork or repairing furniture while you watch a funny movie. It's not multitasking; it's integrating some fun into an otherwise monotonous day of chores, which makes the work go that much faster. Laughter burns calories, too!

- **Remember: the more, the merrier.** Invite your peers or family to join you at a funny movie, an amusing play, or a stand-up comedy performance. Laughter is contagious and is a nonthreatening way to strengthen relationships.

- **Read a funny book.** And share what you read with friends and peers. Write down comic phrases to enjoy again when you feel stressed or to forward in an e-mail to a family member. Your public library and local bookstores are great resources for advice on finding humorous, entertaining books.

- **Be silly.** In a popular episode of the hit television sitcom *Friends*, the character Rachel is aghast at her friend Phoebe's silly method of running helter-skelter, versus the orderly jogging practiced by others at a local park. Rachel ultimately relinquishes her fear of being silly and joins her friend, waving her arms, leaping, and running in a free, unrestrained manner. The point is, it's fun to be silly, so drop your inhibitions sometimes and act silly with a friend or even all by yourself. Sometimes you can have the most fun laughing at yourself.

Burn Calories with a Good Belly Laugh

It's true. Researchers have found that sustained laughter (in other words, a good belly laugh) burns calories.

View Yourself through Your Childhood Eyes

The great scientist Albert Einstein said, "Whoever undertakes to set himself up as a judge of Truth and Knowledge is shipwrecked by the laughter of the gods." As adults, we often take ourselves too seriously, which can prevent us from having more fun in life.

Try this exercise. The next time you find yourself worrying over what someone said at work or whether you will measure up to the expectations of your boss or whether you have adequately responded to all of your e-mails, ask your ten-year-old self what your inner child thinks and then *listen*. Once a client expressed fears that he would not measure up at a technology conference, even though he had spent weeks reading up on the latest advances in computers. I asked him what his response would be if he were ten years old instead of fifty. He said, "Wow! I'll get to see some cool toys." He laughed at the thought, and his anxiety disappeared. Just like that! Sometimes it's enlightening to see yourself through the eyes of your inner child.

Think Back to a Funny Experience or Situation

When you think about it, our lives are full of funny experiences, if we take time to reflect back on them. I remember the day I was walking in the snow with my family and I fell. My daughter couldn't stop laughing. I didn't think it was so funny at the time, but watching her laugh put me into a funny mood as well. What funny experiences can you reflect back on when your stress level starts to climb?

Start Your Own Comedy Night

Gather all of your "funny" friends together, or invite someone who has a "funny gig" to your house and ask that person to try out his or her new material on your crowd. Can you imagine . . . planning a comedy night once a week or every couple of weeks for the mere enjoyment of looking at life's funny side with friends? Just like anything else, you have to plan for it before it happens.

Watch Funny TV Reruns

I often think of the movie *Pretty Woman*, where Julia Roberts plays an adorable prostitute. While she's waiting to go to "work," she amuses herself by watching *I Love Lucy* reruns on television. Some hilarious TV shows are on DVD, such as *Friends*, *Seinfeld*, and others. The main idea here is to spend time every day or each week exercising your "funny" stomach muscles and to downshift your stress level, while you're laughing.

> daily aspiration "I enjoy and appreciate the funny moments and situations in my life today."

9 create boundaries without blaming yourself or others

Today's working moms feel guilty about spending less time with their children, even though research shows that mothers now spend more time with their children than in previous generations. Although the women surveyed by the University of Maryland stated that they didn't spend enough time with their children, the university's researchers discovered that modern-day moms put in more time with their children than mothers did in

1965—an era of the infamously "perfect" TV mom. The study shows that mothers now spend an average of nearly 14.1 hours a week primarily tending to their children, versus 10.2 hours a week in 1965.

This study is an example of how we can experience guilt that is caused by others. In this case, nostalgia about stay-at-home moms in previous generations is pervasive in the mass media, creating guilt where there should be none.

dear diva

"I hate to feel guilty, and I hate being around people who make me feel guilty all the time. It's too overwhelming to have people around you who always want to make you feel bad about yourself. How can I make it stop?"

secrets from the de-stress diva

The guilt you suffer from believing that your actions hurt another person can send your stress levels skyrocketing. Researchers in the United States and Canada report that "great distress" is the result when guilt becomes excessive or irrational. In a situation like this, you can use your emotional intelligence as a powerful weapon against people who make you feel guilty. For example, you may have aging parents who unerringly know how to make you feel guilty about working full-time while raising your children. In this case, use your emotional intelligence to neutralize their criticism. Remind yourself that they might not be aware of the high costs of raising children in this era. In terms of real dollars, the average income in the United States has actually declined since the 1970s. Yet the cost of necessities has skyrocketed.

The American comedian and writer Erma Bombeck put it succinctly: "Guilt, the gift that keeps on giving."

· **Consider the source.** When others *try* to make us feel guilty or we think we *should* be feeling guilty based on others' comments or opinions, ask yourself, Who is trying to make me feel guilty? Is it a sibling, a parent, a colleague, a spouse, or someone else with a specific agenda? Or is something triggering me to feel guilty.

• **Consider the motive.** Once you identify who is trying to make you feel guilty, then you need to figure out the motive behind the guilt-slinging. For example, many people try to control a situation or another person's behavior and use guilt to manipulate someone into doing what they think is correct. Whether people do this intentionally or unintentionally, their motive to control is the same.

What about "mommy guilt" or "can't say no" guilt and many others? An entire industry has sprung up around making moms, spouses, children, and you name it, feel guilty by offering even more extracurricular activities, counseling services, books, and must-have products for mothers and couples than in any previous generation. The media also benefits from the money spent advertising these products and services. Remember, you have the power to control your feelings of guilt.

1. **If you're guilty, admit it and move on.** Don't let guilt rule your thoughts and emotions. If you are accused of something that is wrong, admit your guilt, ask for forgiveness, and move on. Revisiting the scene of the crime does neither party any good; use your mistakes as a learning opportunity. If you are not forgiven, forgive yourself, and move on!

2. **Listen.** If someone is trying to make you feel guilty, ask yourself why. Is it a cry for help or for more attention? Listen "through" the drama to what is actually being said and why. Use your emotional intelligence to learn why someone is trying to make you feel guilty. When you grasp the dynamics of the situation, positively address a way to solve the problem. Many times, this requires direct, heartfelt communication with the person.

3. **Don't be an enabler.** If someone often makes you feel guilty, ask yourself whether you are enabling that person. Don't make guilt the "gift that keeps on giving" for you or other people in your life. If someone is trying to make you feel guilty to get your attention or to control your behavior, try responding with "I want to spend more time with you, *and* I feel pressure from you to . . ."

4. **Make a conscious choice.** Then, consciously choose to spend less time with that person until he or she stops this behavior. You have the power to change from enabler to enlightener.

Breathe

Breathing exercises are a proven stress-buster that can be practiced free of charge, at any time, at work or at home, while you are completing a project, as you do the dishes, while you take a walk, or when you feel anxious or exhausted. If you find yourself in an awkward conversation with someone who is angry or frustrated, spend a few seconds taking deep breaths before you respond.

Always begin and end each day with a deep breathing exercise. Take five deep breaths, exhaling slowly each time. In fact, every time you feel stress, take a series of deep breaths to calm and energize yourself as you breathe in and eliminate the negatives around you as you exhale.

Take a Walk

Walking is a natural de-stressor that works on your emotions as well as your body. On my walks I have come up with some of my best solutions to problems that require sincere and direct communication. I have also thought up many of my most creative programs on my walks. Purchase a pedometer and try to get in ten thousand steps daily. The pedometer can easily be attached to your skirt, pants, or watch, and it automatically tabulates the number of steps you take daily. Just by having the goal of ten thousand steps daily will remind you to keep walking during the day.

Daily Affirmations

Affirmations are an excellent way to assert that we're okay. We sometimes tend to succumb to others' "guilt-making" because we may feel lesser than them, may want to please the other person, or think we'll get extra brownie points if we keep saying yes. Here are a few affirmations that may help you counteract unwanted guilt:

"I honor my time today."
"I love the person I am."
"I have the right to make my own decisions."
"I have confidence in my answers."
"I have the right to say no."

"I have loving boundaries without making the other person wrong."

Practice Saying "No, Thank You!"

One of my friends who has recently retired from a successful placement firm often says, when introducing me to new people, "Ruth is the only person I know who can say no to you and you still feel good about it." When I first heard her say that, I laughed. But then I realized that she meant it, and I reflected on her statement. It became apparent to me that the reason she (and possibly others) may feel that way is because when I do say no to a request or to anything else, I make sure that my refusal comes from a place of compassion for myself and respect for the other person. I know, for example, that when I'm overextended, I'm not a very nice person and that the anxiety and the feelings of being overwhelmed spill into other parts of my life. I don't want that to happen very often, particularly since realizing that I am the one who has the power to say no. I can't blame or control the other person for asking, but I can control my behavior and my words. What freedom I felt when I discovered that!

> daily aspiration   "I honor who I am."

10 are you feeling anxious yet?

The National Institute of Mental Health estimates that forty million Americans, or 18 percent of adults over the age of eighteen, suffer from some form of anxiety disorder at some point in their lives. Anxiety disorders include panic disorder, obsessive-compulsive disorder, post-traumatic stress disorder, generalized anxiety disorder, and phobias (social phobia, agoraphobia, and specific phobias). Help is available if you want to reduce your anxiety.

dear diva

"I have this overall feeling of anxiety with me most of the time, and it causes me a lot of stress. How can I handle my anxiety?"

secrets from the de-stress diva

Anxiety stems from fear, and one of the most important things you can do when you feel anxious is to slow down and breathe. Stephen Price, a recovering agoraphobic and a national public speaker, shares these five tips:

1. **Deepen your breathing.** Learning to control your breathing is the fastest and most basic way to reduce anxiety. That's because your breathing pattern is so closely connected to your emotional state. Rapid, shallow breathing from the top of the lungs is associated with worry, fear, and panic. Slower, deeper breathing that originates in the lower abdomen is associated with a blissful, carefree, and relaxed state.

2. **Change your mental diet.** Self-talk is the diet of the mind. Just as some diets lead to illness and other diets promote health, so it is with the nature of your self-talk. Negative messages are destructive to the mind and cause anxiety, while positive messages heal. Whatever type of messages your mind constantly chews on and digests will profoundly influence your emotional state.

3. **Choose your close relationships carefully.** Like it or not, our closest relationships can cause anxiety or contribute to peace of mind. The problem is that many anxiety sufferers are people-pleasers but choose to have close relationships with people who are difficult to please. These are the people who always place unrealistic expectations on you and withhold their approval unless you meet these expectations.

4. **Schedule a time for worrying.** Cultivate the habit of writing down your worries and make an appointment for worrying each day. This will postpone your anxiety and will help you keep your mind focused on the present.

5. **Exercise! Exercise! Exercise!** A regular running program (or other aerobic exercise) is an excellent way to regulate the physical changes that anxiety produces in your body. It is also the most natural way to satisfy the body's urge to fight or flee.

Each time you go for a run, for example, your body makes use of would-be anxiety symptoms. It needs the extra oxygen from faster breathing, the extra blood flow produced by a rapid heartbeat, and the extra adrenaline for added energy. Plus, after you run, you will enjoy a tired, euphoric feeling brought on by the release of endorphins, the body's natural tranquilizers, into the bloodstream.

Ten Minutes a Day

Dr. Herbert Benson, the director emeritus of the Benson-Henry Institute for Mind Body Medicine at Massachusetts General Hospital, said that setting aside only ten minutes once or twice a day to unwind with yoga, meditation, deep breathing, or even a calming activity like knitting will help you prevent anxiety from taking over. He said, "The repetition breaks the train of everyday thought, and that allows the body and mind to revert to a quiet state."

Schedule One Hour a Day of Worrying

Reserve one hour toward the end of each day for worrying. Keep a notepad with you during the day, and every time you start to worry about something, write it down. Each evening, when the hour comes that you have set aside for worrying, get out your list and focus on each worry, one by one. At the end of the hour, throw away the list and start a fresh one. You will find that some of the worries you wrote down earlier in the day might not seem so serious later that evening.

Write a Letter

A great way to "unload anxiety" is to write a letter to the person who is the cause of the anxious feeling in your mind. Say everything you need to say to this person, and don't hold back on expletives. After it's written, throw it away, burn it, or keep it in your journal . . . but don't send it. This is a wonderfully cathartic experience.

> daily aspiration   "I am breathing in life with calm and peace."

life changes: ready or not

11 starting a new job stress-free

The same "anxiety separation" that children suffer on their first day of school can seize adults on their first day at a new job. This will elevate their stress levels. Some researchers call it "new-job" anxiety. Dr. Melissa Stoppler, a contributor to the *About Stress Management Guide*, reported that the new surroundings, responsibilities, and uncertainties inherent in a new job can combine to become "a significant source of stress."

You can take proactive steps to counter "new-job" anxiety; these include research, planning, organizing, and expressing new-job anxieties openly with friends or loved ones before that first day at a new workplace.

dear diva

"I'm so nervous about my new job I can't sleep. What if I can't deliver what I promised during the interview? What if I'm too old or unequipped to get up to speed with everyone else? What if no one likes me? How can I start my new job the positive, no-stress way?"

secrets from the de-stress diva

1. **Be prepared.** Before you start your new job, do your homework. Research your company's history. Read a copy of the latest one or two annual reports. Familiarize yourself with the names and the titles of your future supervisors and coworkers.

2. **Be rested.** Eat healthy foods and sleep well every night, so that you arrive at work looking and feeling your best. A healthy diet and sound sleep will also help to lessen your anxieties in the days before you start the new job.

3. **Be early.** Arriving a few minutes early during your first week of work will allow you extra time to prepare for the days ahead, while also signaling that you are enthusiastic about your new position. If you are nervous, arriving early will give you a few extra minutes to orient yourself to your new surroundings and to relax and focus.

4. **Be organized.** Organize your schedule at the start of every day. Add to your notes each time you meet someone new, to incorporate that person's name and title into your to-do list of things to remember.

5. **Be proactive.** Find a project you can begin and complete within the first few weeks or the first month to show that you can tackle a project and also to prove to yourself that you can accomplish a goal quickly. Just don't pick too tough of a project; instead, pick one that incorporates and showcases the skills you bring to the job.

6. **Be ready to learn.** Every new job comes with a learning curve. Regardless of how many years you have spent in your field, be ready to learn a new fact, a new technology, a new skill, or a new approach. Stay calm and persist.

7. **Be positive.** Smile at every opportunity. Say please and thank you often. Being positive goes a long way toward establishing you as a person whom others will be eager to help and to work with.

8. **Ask.** If you don't know, ask. Don't pretend that you know how to do something or know who to approach if you don't. Ask for help.

9. **Be professional.** When deciding what to wear, err on the conservative side, rather than dressing casually. You'll make a better impression. When engaged in conversation, follow your new coworkers' lead in how to address people. If you don't know their titles, ask.

10. **Leave on time.** Leaving long after office hours are over signals that you don't have a good grasp of what you should know. Leave on time; just don't leave early.

Breathe

You can de-stress, on the spot, without anyone else knowing that you are anxious, if you practice calming breathing exercises. Whether you are at your desk, walking down a hallway, or in the middle of a conversation, you can internally slow your breathing. Breathe in slowly; exhale slowly. This will calm you and also energize you by carrying more oxygen to your body and your brain.

Aromatherapy

Here are a few maladies caused by stress and the essential oils that will help you to downshift:

Mental stress: basil, various types of citrus, and neroli essential oils

Emotional stress: sandalwood and lavender essential oils

Think *Big*

Oftentimes, we tend to think "small." I would like you to think *big* in terms of your opportunities, your capabilities, and your venture into this new job. When fear or stress gets the best of you, think expansively as if expecting *big* things from the world. Think of the universe as a *big* resource center that will provide everything you need.

daily aspiration   "I have so many wonderful opportunities ahead of me."

12 changing careers: now what?

Workplace stress is epidemic, and dozens of medical studies have confirmed that stress on the job can lead to dangerous physical conditions, ranging from obesity and high blood pressure to diabetes and life-threatening heart attacks. The emotional toll can wreak permanent damage on marriages; on relationships with friends, children, and family; and on your emotional well-being. For many people, changing careers is not only about changing their lifestyles, but about protecting the quality of their lives.

dear diva

"I hate my job, and I'm too exhausted to look for another since I work eighty hours a week. I'm angry and resentful, tired, and I feel ill. If I leave my job, I'm afraid I'll never find another. I'm making myself sick thinking about all of this, and it's already time to go back to work. Should I change careers?"

secrets from the de-stress diva

Longer work hours and lower pay, when inflation is factored in, mean that more people are working longer and harder for less money, and with less job security or benefits. Fewer people are taking vacations, adding to the nonstop stress, and the lack of universal health care means that most stress-related conditions are going untreated.

1. **Tap into your inner childhood.** Changing careers can be fun, really, if you tap into your inner childhood. When you were a child, you were often asked what you wanted to be when you grew up. Ask your inner child this same question, and let your inner child answer. Do this. Rent a copy of the lighthearted Disney film *The Kid*, starring Bruce Willis, and watch it with your inner child. You'll find yourself beginning to believe that changing careers can be fun! Don't embark on this journey with a highly stressed, unhappy state of mind. If you make "having fun" your goal, this is ultimately a more productive way to approach your new career.

2. **Create an action plan.** Take proactive steps to put yourself in charge of your career, instead of living with the high stress that comes with not controlling your own destiny. If you are unhappy with your job and find that you cannot make changes that will allow you to be happier at that job, then decide right now to change jobs, and get started on an action plan. Create a chart on paper. Give yourself a week to research career-change options. Ask yourself, What am I truly interested in doing in my work and in my life? During week two, whittle down your findings to one or two potential careers, then "go deep" for the following week by exploring the pluses and the minuses of each one. Next, start looking, and chart your progress as you go. Changing jobs and careers is not instantaneous; allow yourself the time and the patience that you will need to find a truly rewarding new career.

3. **Network.** Networking is still the most powerful way to find a rewarding job. If you are changing careers, then expand your professional networks to zero in on the career you really want. Invest in a membership at your local chamber of commerce, and join committees or subgroups related to your next career, not to your current one.

Integrate Your Lifestyle Goals

Don't merely think about changing careers; plan how you can reach your lifestyle goals, while incorporating your career change. For example, if you want to spend more time with your family, consider changing to a career that might pay less but that provides the priceless dividend of time. Vow to simplify your life to live within a smaller budget to reach your lifestyle goal. If you want to be healthier, consider changing to a career that does not force you to sit at a desk for ten hours a day. Remember, it's better to downsize your budget than to resign yourself to having an unhappy, shorter life.

Create a Career Change SWAT Team

Enlist your friends and trusted peers into your own Career Change SWAT Team. Let them know that you want to change careers, and ask for their suggestions and their help. Every person has a unique circle of acquaintances. Ask each friend to consult with his or her circle to gather more expert advice that will help you reach your goal.

Organize

To change careers, you must organize your time to allow yourself one hour each day to focus on the career change. Make a schedule and stick to it, devoting one hour each day to career research, networking, or other responsibilities that will lead you to your new destination in life. Simplify chores, meals, and other responsibilities to create this extra hour in your day.

Visualize

There is a point of light located in the center of your forehead. Many people call this your "third eye," and it represents the core of your intuition. Visualize and meditate for five to ten minutes each day to become inspired about your career.

> daily aspiration   "I love my new career."

✦13 delegating is a good thing

Outsourcing has captured the imaginations of most working professionals, especially with the advent of technology and the availability of "virtual" assistants who can work for you through the Internet without your incurring the expense of renting office space. Today, through the Internet, you can create a virtual staff by using the services of individuals or companies that are not necessarily located in your state or even country. You can literally go anywhere online to find the best help for the right price to fit your specific needs and your budget.

According to the International Virtual Assistants Association, almost every business of any size has benefited from using virtual assistants for bookkeeping, writing, editing, graphic design, public relations, media relations, strategic planning, and technical and creative services. You can't do everything yourself, and trying to do so will create stress, while also diverting your attention from the tasks you do best. That's why even solo entrepreneurs use the same outsourcing strategies that major international firms do, to boost their bottom line.

dear diva

"I have too much to do and not enough time to do it all. Please help."

secrets from the de-stress diva

1. **Delegate.** Make a list of what you do best, and delegate as many of your other responsibilities as possible by outsourcing. Make a "to delegate" list based on what will best free up your time so that you can accomplish your main goals. For example, think of daily activities that you consider tedious and time-consuming as areas where you can use outsourced help. Keep a running list of your outsourced work and your virtual assistants. For example, I have created a form (you can download it at www.destressdiva.com/assistants) that allows you to keep a list of what each assistant needs to do and also provides an easy way for you to manage what has or hasn't been done.

2. **Create a detailed job description.** Before you outsource, create a detailed job description listing the skills and the work you want done. Use this to advertise for outsourced help.

3. **Audition your help.** Allow candidates to audition for the job by performing a task you want accomplished as their audition, such as writing, analysis of a project, and so forth.

4. **Measure their contributions.** Create a to-do list for your out-sourced help, and require your virtual staff members to submit a "done" list with each invoice. You'll be able to better track their progress and will have a resource to analyze over time to determine whether your outsourcing needs are being met or you need to look elsewhere.

5. **Be flexible.** It takes time to develop an off-site relationship. Allow your outsourced help and yourself enough time to synchronize different time zones, personalities, and styles of delivery to accommodate your needs.

6. **Be considerate.** The 24/7 availability of the Internet does not mean you can expect 24/7 access to your virtual staff. Keep different time zones in mind. Don't expect an e-mail that you send at 2 P.M. to be answered at 2:15 A.M. Just as onsite staff members can have emergencies that keep them from the office, so can your virtual assistant. Make sure, however, that these "emergencies" do not happen repeatedly.

7. **Protect your intellectual assets.** Consult an intellectual assets specialist to ensure that your assets do not become those of your virtual assistant. An attorney can create a contract that protects your trade secrets, methods for accomplishing work, unique products and services, and other intellectual assets.

Glance at Your Calendar

Our calendars are wonderful sources for information. In this case, I want you to start gathering information about how your time is being used.

1. Look at your calendar to figure out how you have been spending your time.

2. Ask yourself, "Is this where I want to be spending my time and energy?"

3. Reflect back on week one and try to remember whether you felt stressed, overwhelmed, or calm and how much high-priority work was accomplished.

Write

Write about what you would like to spend your time doing at work and at home. Just keep writing until you have about three pages of notes. It usually takes two pages before your subconscious desires clearly begin to emerge.

Check Personalities

To lower your stress when working with a virtual assistant, you may want to choose your assistant just as you would any employee, making sure that her or his skills are what you need and that your personalities are compatible.

Breathe

According to the *Journal of Human Hypertension*, you can potentially lower your blood pressure by slowing your breathing to fewer than ten breaths per minute, for about ten minutes, and this may lower your blood pressure 5 to 10 points.

Laugh

For as little as fifteen minutes a day, you can burn up to 40 calories by laughing, reported the *International Journal of Obesity*. Laughter also promotes stress relief and strengthens the immune system.

Virtual Assistants Resources

www.craigslist.org is an online area where you can place your ad for the type of employee and work you are looking for.
www.assistu.com is a site where you will find qualified virtual assistants in many different areas of expertise.

daily aspiration   "I give myself permission to delegate work today."

14 surviving hot flashes and the great transition

As the baby boomers did with rock and roll music and women's liberation, the most influential generation of our times has also led the way in making women more knowledgeable about menopause and its precursor, perimenopause. The baby boomers have paved the way for younger women who are now approaching this transition, as is evident by hundreds of books and Web sites and thousands of articles focused on what happens to women's bodies when their menstrual cycles end. The natural decline in ovarian function that marks the start of menopause is a time when women become freed from the expense and the discomfort of monthly periods. It's also a time when the stress of daily life for women of any age can exacerbate hot flashes, weight gain, and other symptoms of menopause. High levels of stress, in fact, can trigger early menopause, as well as perimenopause—a prelude to menopause that can include many of the same symptoms as menopause, even as women continue to have their periods. We are also living in an era when more women are joining the workforce and continuing to work in their fifties and sixties, which translates into having to take those hot flashes with them to the office.

dear diva

"I'm burning up with hot flashes, and I find myself barking at people over the littlest things. I don't think I can take this anymore. How can I get through menopause the healthy way?"

secrets from the de-stress diva

In America's youth-oriented culture, which ironically has larger numbers of people who are past fifty than most other countries, menopause has become as traumatic as wrinkles and graying hair for some women. "Denial," as Mark Twain once put it, "ain't just a river in Egypt." Get a grip, girls!

I've talked to too many clients who fear that their male coworkers will react negatively if they witness a little sweat on the women's brows—a natural symptom of the temperature fluctuations more commonly known as "hot flashes"—in the middle of a business meeting. If this worries you, it may be time for a reality check. Most men, who have lived in close proximity with sisters, mothers, girlfriends, wives, and daughters who regularly bleed once a month, can handle a little perspiration on the forehead. Honest. If you have a husband, he'd rather watch you turn beet red several times a day than turn beet red himself at the thought of having to go to the drugstore to pick up a box of tampons or that great big box of sanitary napkins for you. So, stop stressing!

eight smart tips to get you through menopause

1. **Don't think menopause; think "power surge."** In fact, that's the title of a delightfully enlightening Web site at www.power-surge.com that has offered smart information and "live" online chats with veteran physicians, nutritionists, and other experts for the last fifteen years. If you're going through menopause, bookmark this page.

2. **Power up with knowledge.** What your mother didn't tell you is plenty. There is more information about menopause and perimenopause than was available for your mother's generation, so take advantage of the many books, Web sites, articles, and scientific journals that focus on this topic. Ask your physician and your librarian for suggestions on books and articles that would best serve you. We all go through menopause differently, with different attitudes and symptoms.

3. **Take your calcium.** Take all of your vitamins, but pay special attention to calcium since menopause also occurs at a time when women begin to suffer the most from bone loss. The bonus is that new research suggests that a glass of nonfat milk each day is also important for weight control. Women who drink milk every day tend to weigh less than women who don't.

4. **Exercise.** Exercise is not only good for fighting the extra weight gain that tends to come with menopause and the

more sedentary lives of aging people; it also reduces the stress and even the panic attacks caused by the substantial hormonal changes that accompany menopause.

5. **Throw out the junk food.** Junk food often contains the very ingredients that can worsen hot flashes and other symptoms of menopause. Toss out the cookies, and eat more fruit and foods containing fiber.

6. **Write off your worries.** By that, I mean write them down on a piece of paper and throw them away, or write down your worries in a journal and then close the book. Keeping a journal is also a useful way to track your symptoms and thus proactively address when and how your menopausal symptoms occur.

7. **Get a menopause buddy.** Enlist a friend who is undergoing menopause. Make it a point to spend time with each other every week to vent your frustrations and encourage each other through this transition. There really is strength in numbers, especially on an emotional level. Laugh together! It's a stress-buster, and it makes you feel younger.

8. **Educate your family and friends.** Let them know that you are going through menopause and that you want their support. Understanding is a powerful weapon against stress. Let your loved ones know what to expect, and they will be there to help you through menopause.

About Those Hot Flashes

Here are a few quick tips to help you through that next hot flash:

- Drink a glass of cold water at the onset of a hot flash.
- Keep bags of frozen vegetables in your freezer at home. Place a bag on your face, neck, inner arms, or wrists to quickly cool that hot flash. If no one's looking, place a bag of frozen peas on top of your head if that's what it takes!
- Think cotton. It's a fabric that breathes, which will make you feel cool and comfortable when you wear cotton clothing and sleep on cotton sheets.

- Time the duration of your hot flashes. Once you know roughly how many minutes they last, you can be ready to excuse yourself for those few minutes to cool your wrists at the sink or take a refreshing walk.
- Relax your mind and your muscles.

Sage Leaf Tea

Steep one teaspoon of fresh sage leaves in a cup of hot (boiling) water for four to five minutes. Strain it, and drink one or two cups of this tea a day.

Sexual Activity

Dr. Stephanie Dolds, the head doctor from Integrative Medicine Associates, said that "sexual intercourse does the body good" and releases oxytocin, a hormone that helps women get through menopause and lowers stress. Sex is one of the best and healthiest ways to lower stress for women . . . and men!

Aromatherapy

10 drops lemon oil
5 drops peppermint oil
2 drops clary sage oil

Add the oils to 1 ounce aloe vera gel. Shake, stir, or blend to mix everything together. Dab or spray the mixture on your wrists, face, or neck whenever a hot flash threatens to hit.

(Source: Kathi Keville, *Aromatherapy for Dummies*)

> daily aspiration "I embrace all new opportunities."

15 moving made easy

If you feel stressful at the thought of moving, you're not alone. About 19 percent of the U.S. population moves every year. And, according to the Employee Relocation Council, moving is third only behind death and divorce as the most stressful life event.

Moving disrupts routines, lifestyles, and friendships and uproots families. Moving is physically exhausting. The anxieties of moving to a strange neighborhood, city, state, or country can become overwhelming when you factor in the high cost of moving.

dear diva

"I'm so exhausted at the transition from job to job, how do I find the energy to start packing boxes, and how will I afford it? I'm being forced to move because of a new job, and my family resents this. How can I make my move less stressful?"

secrets from the de-stress diva

1. **Start planning now.** Start to make moving plans the day you know that you will be moving. Create a to-do calendar. Call the utility companies. Fill out your change-of-address cards. Call for estimates from moving companies. Tell friends and family members to expect a call from you soon to help you move.

2. **Do the math.** The high cost of moving is a huge stress instigator. Do the math upfront to minimize your stress. Spend a few hours putting together a moving budget, and then stick to it. Remember that replacing household items is sometimes less expensive than moving them. Throwing out or donating unused items immediately will save you the expense of packing, moving, and re-storing them. Plus, you earn a charitable deduction for donated items.

3. **Simplify.** Delegate moving chores to each person in your house, choosing taskmasters by their individual talents. For example, let the cleaning master do all the cleaning. Let the household mechanic make sure that everything is taken apart and packed so that it can be easily put together again. Break down complex moving chores into simple jobs.

4. **De-clutter.** Moving can be a time of sadness, regrets, or anger when you sort through possessions that can evoke these negative feelings. You have another choice, however, to see moving as an opportunity to reorganize your priorities and anticipate new adventures. Throw away belongings that carry negative emotional baggage. Toss out items that will slow you down if you have to clean, store, or preserve them for several more years. Now is the time to carefully preserve and restore cherished objects that you want to pass down to your children and relatives after you are gone. Mark them to be stored in a safe, dry place. Is anything else really necessary? If it's not, throw it away.

5. **Label everything.** For each box you pack, tape a piece of paper to the outside on which you have listed the contents, item by item. It will save you time and stress when you are unpacking. Color-code the packing boxes by rooms. For example, place a green dot (with a sticker or a green marker) on each box from your kitchen and a red dot on each box containing items from your bedroom. Did you know that you can buy large wardrobe boxes from moving truck companies? These boxes are sturdy and a good place to pack sofa cushions, bedding, toys, or outdoor goods.

6. **Clean as you go.** Every time you pack up a room, take a packing break by stopping to thoroughly clean that room. Then close the door to measure your progress. Ditto with each closet, refrigerator, and other measurable space in your house.

7. **Enlist outside help.** If you can afford it, pay a cleaning company, rather than exhausting yourself to the point of becoming dangerously fatigued. Enlist friends or family members to help you plan, move, and unpack. Enlist sitters for your children or pets on moving day or unpacking day.

8. **Anticipate positives.** Instead of worrying about the loss of old friends, neighborhoods, and habits, anticipate new friends, new hobbies or skills you can learn, and new places for adventure. Take a break from moving to investigate museums, libraries, parks, and other fun places in the vicinity of your new home, and engage your family in discussions about the benefits of your new place while you are still moving from your old place. Plan to reward everyone for a successful move with activities that involve your new home.

Fatigue Fighters

Few things are more fatiguing than moving. Here are a few fatigue fighters you can incorporate into your move or do when you're ready to take a quick break:

- **Eat well.** Healthy meals diminish fatigue by supplying the vitamins, the minerals, the proteins, and the liquids that your body needs for maximum energy. Be sure to take a multivitamin as a backup during stressful periods of your life such as when you are moving.
- **Stretch.** Stretching often will make your body more limber and less susceptible to injury, especially when you are lifting, pushing, and moving.
- **Laugh.** Laughter is exercise, in and of itself, and can provide a healthy release of tension during stressful moves. Play a funny recording when packing with family members or friends or by yourself. You'll be more likely to laugh than cry when you drop and break something. Reward yourself at the end of a busy moving day with a trip to the theater to see a funny movie.
- **Rest.** Packing day and night will ultimately exhaust you by depriving you of sleep. No matter what your moving schedule is, make it a priority to get seven to eight hours of sleep every night. No excuses. Plus, a well-rested you won't scare your new neighbors, as you might if you show up grouchy with dark circles under your eyes.
- **Reward yourself.** At the end of every few days or each week of packing and moving, reward yourself with a special meal or event or merely a night off. Plan your rewards in advance so that you can anticipate a positive, fun activity at the end of each segment of your packing, moving, and unpacking.

Stretch Out Your Back

Bring your arms above your head as you inhale and slowly bend forward from the waist to hang down, stretching your back, neck, and arms. Do this several times during the day while you are packing and moving.

Bathe with Epsom Salts

A great way to relax your sore muscles after a day of packing or moving is to take a warm bath with a few teaspoons of Epsom salts in your bath water. Enjoy!

> daily aspiration   "I am entering a new and adventurous time of my life."

16 pregnancy-proof your life

Being pregnant can be one of the most joyous periods in a woman's life. But when you have a baby growing inside of you, you're also bound to feel some stress—it's only natural. After all, every mother desperately wants her child to be born healthy. And besides that, your body is thrown completely out of whack, and those biological changes can trigger stress and discomfort. But the good news is, there are many steps you can take to soothe yourself.

dear diva

"I'm not sleeping well because I'm uncomfortable and there are so many things I need to do to get ready for this baby. How can I better manage my preparations for the baby?"

secrets from the de-stress diva

- Start by not putting too much pressure on yourself, physically or emotionally. Don't think that you have to be the perfect pregnant mom and have every single thing ready in the baby's room by the time your little one is born or that you must research every potential medical problem on the Internet or cross off each item on your pregnancy to-do list every day.

- Tell yourself this on a regular basis: "My baby won't notice if I don't get everything done. My baby won't care if we put some finishing touches on his/her room after he/she is born."

- Don't try to shoulder all of your anxieties by yourself. If certain medical questions are worrying you, write them down and ask your doctor about these issues, either on the phone or during an appointment. Your physician can put your worries to rest. And if your doctor makes you feel as if you're bothering him or her, you should think about switching doctors.

- During this time, many people may want to give you pregnancy and parenting advice. Don't feel overwhelmed or think that you have to take everything in. You'll figure things out as you go along—that's part of what makes the journey so exciting.

- And don't *ever* let anyone's criticism, even a well-meaning remark, make you feel bad about yourself.

- Pamper yourself during this time. Be kind and comforting to your body. It's under a lot of pressure, so make it feel better.

- Exercise regularly. This will improve your mental health and make you sleep much more soundly. Always check with your doctor first, however.

- Prenatal yoga provides a relaxing, calming workout. Call a local yoga studio or get a prenatal yoga DVD and do it at home. Again, check with your doctor before starting any exercise routine.

- Eat well. Focus on healthy, nutritious foods, and don't skip meals. In fact, have frequent small meals.

- Do something nice for yourself every day. Meet a friend for a long lunch, have a movie date with your husband, go on a shopping outing with a girlfriend, or take a luxurious soak in the tub while you read a magazine.

- Do some journaling; reflecting on your feelings and writing them down can be very helpful. Purchase a diary or a pregnancy notebook and record your thoughts at different intervals during these nine months. Make it a peaceful routine that you look forward to. Write during the quiet of night, or perhaps before you go to bed, with soft music playing in the background, if that helps you to concentrate.

- Think positively and be mindful of wondrous moments in your everyday life. Treasure them.

- Practice meditation and visual imaging. Visualize yourself serenely cradling your baby and loving him or her.
- Sit in a comfortable position and practice deep breathing. Put your hands on your belly and feel your breathing. This can be very relaxing. Deep breathing and relaxation exercises might also come in handy for your labor and delivery.

> daily aspiration   "I'm doing something fantastic and miraculous just by carrying a baby in my womb."

17 weddings

Weddings are supposed to be joyous occasions, but more often they become a source of unrelenting stress. Money is the chief culprit, according to numerous surveys showing that the high cost of weddings tops marital compatibility, in-laws, and other topics of concern. One survey by Condé Nast found that the average wedding can cost $27,000 and upward. A recent American Express nationwide survey of five hundred newlyweds found that almost all of them—80 percent—felt that the financial side of planning for their wedding was stressful. No wonder the wedding business is a $72 million industry! The American Express study also found that 75 percent of the newlyweds surveyed either did not set up a wedding budget or did not stick to their budget.

dear diva

"This wedding is going to be so stressful and so expensive, I don't know how to get through it. I'm ready to scream at all the bad advice I'm getting from everyone, and I feel more frustrated every day. How can I make my wedding a joyous, not stressful, event?"

secrets from the de-stress diva

1. **Set your true goals.** Is your true goal to impress the neighbors with an expensive wedding or to marry the person you love? One involves peer pressure and the other involves personal feelings. Vow to follow your personal goals, and use that as your compass when planning your wedding.

2. **Set a budget and stick to it.** Create a budget, and then stick to it. Period. There are great, free online wedding budget–planning charts that can help you, such as the free "wedding budgeter" chart at www.theknot.com.

3. **Delegate.** To stick to your budget, choose a friend or a relative to be in charge of managing the finances for certain expenses, such as the meal, the dress, or other items on your list. Delegating the chore of budgeting a wedding expense will not only help you to save time, but will also help you to stick to your overall budget.

4. **Keep it simple.** Lavish weddings can be a great source of discomfort, not only for your budget, but also for your guests. Choose intimate over grand, and you'll have a wedding that's truly personal. As you create your wedding budget, ask yourself with every item, "How can I simplify this?" Then do so.

   If you want to have a wedding at an expensive resort, skydive from a plane, and eat caviar, break it down. Have a simple wedding, and honeymoon at a resort. Choose a simple menu for your wedding, and promise yourself an extravagant meal at a restaurant on your first anniversary. Don't make your wedding the one place to fulfill all of your wedding dreams; make it the first step to fulfilling a lifetime of dreams.

5. **Celebrate, don't obligate.** Don't make your guests feel as if they are also obliged to become victims of financial stress because of your wedding. Ask yourself, How can I make this wedding a celebration, not an obligation, for my friends and family? For example, don't register at expensive stores if most of your friends are social workers or teachers, even if your relatives are rich.

   In fact, ask your smartest, kindest friend to serve as your informal gift counselor, instead of giving you a gift. Then, ask relatives and friends to refer guests to your gift counselor, who can offer practical suggestions, but who is also ready to say that a handwritten

card can be a more thoughtful and prized gift than anything purchased. If you ask older couples, they will confirm that handmade,
handwritten cards and presents and personal photographs have
become dearer to them than forgotten gifts from their long-ago
wedding.

6. **Breathe.** Every time you feel the stress of peer pressure infringing
on your wedding plans, step away and breathe deeply, in and out.
Take a calming or brisk walk to energize and refocus yourself. Eat
healthy foods, and sleep well. Good health is a powerful deterrent
against stress so cultivate healthy habits long before, as well as
during, this important event.

> daily aspiration   "I will always love my husband/wife."

18 the great divide: how to survive divorce

Numerous studies on death and divorce have found that
divorce can be more dangerous to your long-term physical
and emotional health than even the death of a spouse. In death,
the end of the relationship is confirmed. With divorce, the sur-
vival of the spouse can often lead to a failure to admit and accept
the end of the marriage. Certainly, the death rates for divorced
men are higher than those for married men. Other studies show
that divorce can also wreak emotional and physical damage on
children of the broken marriage, which creates new levels of
stress for divorced parents who feel guilty about this.

dear diva

"I'm afraid that the whole world knows I'm a failure because I'm
getting a divorce. My children hate me, and I have so much anger
inside, it's hard to think. I don't know how I'll get through this. How
can I survive my divorce?"

secrets from the de-stress diva

1. **Think of new beginnings, not endings.** The end of something can also mark the beginning of something new. By focusing on what comes after the divorce, you'll reset your mind to begin thinking about new goals. Write several new goals in your journal, and revisit your journal every time you begin to feel stress from your divorce.

2. **Grieve.** The grieving process is more acceptable for widows and widowers than for the divorced, but it is just as important for those undergoing divorce. Create a "grieving support system" from among your friends or relatives, and set aside time to grieve with them. When you grieve alone, recognize and accept that this is a natural condition and will pass. In this way, you will not become stressed when you grieve. If you have no support system, then join a support system in your community. Don't become a victim of grief; if you must, schedule a time of day to grieve to allow yourself to accept that the divorce will happen and also to prevent grief from taking over your life.

3. **Be healthy.** The high stress levels caused by divorce can weaken your immune system and may result in unhealthy eating and sleeping habits. Keep yourself healthy and strong for the next stage in your life by getting enough sleep and eating nutritious foods. Exercise often. Exercise is a great stress-buster to use anytime, including before or after you meet with your former spouse or with attorneys or interact with your children. Stress is contagious.

4. **Ask for help.** If you broke your leg, you wouldn't just wrap it with a bandage and go back to your desk. Divorce can take a far worse emotional and physical toll. In fact, use the broken leg example when you explain to others why you want help, because it is the sensible, healthy thing to do. Whether you use personal support systems of family or friends, seek professional guidance from a mental practitioner, or get help from a community support group, recognize that help is available. Just ask!

5. **Create a support system for your children.** Make sure that your children survive the stress of divorce, too, by creating a support system for them. Invite favorite relatives to become support teams for your children, whether they live in the neighborhood or can be available for regularly scheduled, long-distance phone calls.

Let school counselors know that your children are going through a divorce, so that they can understand and respond more intelligently to any changes in your children's behavior. Tell your children it's okay to be sad, but also encourage them to focus on new things that will happen in their lives.

6. **Pamper yourself.** Use your emotional intelligence to recognize that divorce is stressful for everyone, everywhere, and resolve to pamper yourself. Treat yourself often to fun trips with your children, which can be as inexpensive as a picnic outside a local museum or at a public park in a different neighborhood. Take a course at a community college on a topic that has always interested you. Indulge yourself in long walks, happy reunions, funny movies, and a dinner out with a wonderful friend. Create a list of fun things (free things, if you are on a budget) to do each week, either alone or with your family or friends.

Find the Spark of Hope

In every type of adversity there is a spark of hope, a glimmer of optimism that at first is usually hidden from view. Visualize a spark of life reminding you of all of your talents and abilities and the depth of love you have in your life . . . and use this spark to help you see the road ahead, even if the spark casts only enough light for you to take one step at a time.

Aromatherapy

In her book *The Aromatherapy Companion*, Victoria H. Edwards puts together an aromatherapy blend "to combat negative thoughts that deplete feminine energy." Her formula is:

2 ounces grapeseed oil
1 ounce apricot oil
1 ounce macadamia, avocado, or rose hip oil
Lavender essential oil
Geranium essential oil
Sweet marjoram essential oil
Clary sage essential oil
Blue chamomile essential oil

Mix the first three carrier oils in a 4-ounce dark glass bottle, and add a total of twenty to thirty drops of a combination of the essential oils.

To use: After a shower or a bath, lightly towel yourself dry, and, while your pores are still open, apply the oil. Start at your feet and work upward. The oil will mix with the water that's left on the surface of your skin to form a creamy lotion.

Food

Elizabeth Andes-Bell, a yoga instructor in New York, suggests the following:

- Drink at least one glass of freshly squeezed green juice per day (chard, cucumber, celery, apple, and lemon). It's a great alkalizer and detoxifier.
- Drink alkaline, filtered water.
- Eat all-organic fruits and veggies; no white flour, sugar, dairy, meat, or processed foods.
- Carry organic tea bags and stevia (a sugar substitute) for a healthy alternative when everyone else is having lattés.

Yoga

Elizabeth Andes-Bell suggests recapitulation, which is a Mexican shamanic technique for dealing with someone with whom you have an ongoing difficult relationship (family member, spouse, ex, coworker, and so forth).

Shamanic traditions emphasize the accumulation and the mastery of personal energy as the key to empowerment. Close your eyes and visualize the person. How do you feel with that individual? Energized or drained? Work only with people who drain or suck your life force.

- Stand up, feet on the floor, with your knees slightly bent.
- Breathe slowly and fully. Place your fingertips on your belly two inches below your navel. This is your power point. Breathe into this point and imagine a glowing ball of orange light. Feel your own power increase as you breathe.

- Visualize the person before you, standing face-to-face with you. Say, "I forgive you and honor your essence. I honor my essence and take back my life energy for the greater good."
- Scoop up your life energy and return it to your own power point.
- Journal your feelings about the experience. Notice what evolves over time. You may want to repeat this regularly with a particularly challenging situation.

> daily aspiration   "I am whole, I am enough, and I am lovable just the way I am."

the workplace

19 traffic jams

Researchers report that traffic congestion during the commute to and from work is often the biggest source of stress. Numerous studies have found a direct correlation between heavy traffic and higher blood pressure and unhealthy levels of stress hormones. Hence, the incidence of "road rage" is on the rise, contributing to more accidents.

Meanwhile, the increasing use of cell phones is creating another danger on the road. Some studies show that cell phone users are four times more likely to be in an accident, which has led most European countries to ban cell phone use while driving. The United States is beginning to take heed, with four states and Washington, D.C., already banning the practice, and several others now considering similar laws.

Even if using a cell phone while driving is not against the law where you live, don't do it. Keep in mind that headsets or other hands-free driving devices don't reduce accidents because, as researchers at Virginia Tech and Johns Hopkins University have found, it is the cell phone conversation itself that is dangerous. The researchers proved in separate surveys that when you are talking, the conversation overwhelms the part of the brain that controls your visual skills.

dear diva

"I dread getting into my car, knowing that I'll be sitting in traffic with mean, thoughtless drivers on either side of me and knowing that I'll have to do the same thing when I'm finished at work. I am so stressed, I feel like screaming at the bad driver in front of me. How can I keep myself from going nuts when I'm in traffic?"

secrets from the de-stress diva

1. **Leave earlier in the morning.** Don't make yourself a victim of rush-hour jams in the morning. If you can't convince your employer to

change your arrival time, move the clock up to arrive an hour or even two hours early. Use this time to exercise by taking a forty-five-minute energizing walk, and then start your day in the office a few minutes early to organize your day's priorities. Exercising or even visiting a like-minded friend for an early, healthy breakfast is more productive and less stressful than sitting in traffic.

2. **Leave work later.** You can also postpone your departure time from the office to avoid the usual rush-hour snarl. Take a course at a nearby community college, or spend an hour at the local library updating your skills or studying a subject you love. Plan an after-work get-together with friends once a week to take a break from sitting in traffic.

3. **Relax.** When you find yourself in unavoidable traffic jams, breathe deeply, in and out, to calm yourself and focus your attention on the road. Road rage can provoke the same response from other drivers, so don't become a victim of escalating anger. If a driver in your lane or behind you acts too aggressively, escape via the nearest exit and reenter the roadway later to keep yourself safe.

4. **Learn.** Use books on tape or books on CD to distract or entertain yourself or to learn new things while you are sitting in traffic. Over time, you can pick up a new language this way or inspire yourself with motivational recordings.

5. **Don't talk on your cell phone.** Cell phones are becoming a major cause of traffic accidents, which is why many cities have banned their use on the road or are now considering doing so. Text messaging can prove even more disastrous. Don't do it. Keep your cell phone for emergency use only and pull over to the side of the road to make that call. If you are waiting for an important phone call, ask yourself this: "Is it worth risking my life to answer that call?" Don't do it.

6. **Accept being late.** Sometimes, unexpected traffic can make you late. When it's convenient, pull to the side of the road to call in your apologies on your cell phone. (Never do this while you are behind the wheel.) Look at all of the drivers on your crowded roadway and realize that they are late, too. It's part of life, so accept it instead of being stressed out.

7. **Consider mass transit.** In this era of global warming, it's as environmentally responsible (and trendy!) as it is practical, cost-effective, and less stressful to take a bus, a train, a trolley, or a subway. Or you

could car pool. Instead of dreading getting behind the wheel, you'll look forward to letting someone else do the driving while you read a good book or an interesting magazine, plot your day's schedule on paper, or just mentally de-stress.

Listen to Music

If you want to relax during your drive, then listen to soft music. If you want to wake up during a morning or an afternoon drive, listen to upbeat music. It is amazing how people are influenced by sound.

Shoulder Rolls at Light Signals

Try rolling your shoulders forward three times and then backward three times. Do this repetition until the light changes. This is a great way to relax your neck and shoulder muscles and helps you to de-stress.

Before You Belt Up

Pause for a few minutes to say an affirmation for the day or before going to lunch . . . whenever you're in the car and ready to go somewhere.

Your affirmations may be something like these:

"I am driving safely and calmly to . . . "

"I am grateful for this car that takes me where I want to go when I want to."

"I am looking forward to arriving home to see my family."

daily aspiration   "My life is so much easier with my car."

20 start your workday stress-free

High stress on the job can sabotage efforts to increase productivity because it can lead to higher rates of absences, illnesses, and job turnover, which are major contributors to the annual $300 billion cost of workplace stress for today's employers. TimeManagementTraining.com reports that 50 percent of management time is spent processing information, and 80 percent of that information is of no value. Thus, it is vital to take control of the data flow to focus only on the most important information.

dear diva

"When I arrive at work, my stress goes through the roof. New work is piled on top of work I have not yet finished. Phones are ringing, and there are dozens of e-mails waiting to be read. I feel overwhelmed before I get started. How do I make my mornings at work less stressful and more productive?"

secrets from the de-stress diva

Starting your workday can be stressful and unproductive if you don't get organized. Here are five fast ways to get organized and stay organized throughout your day to stave off stress and maximize your productivity.

1. **Start your day the stress-free way.** Before tuning in to the morning news or turning on your computer to check your e-mail, spend the first ten minutes of your day stretching, meditating, and silently thinking about the day ahead. It's a stress-free beginning that will prove more productive than immediately falling into "overwhelmed." Skipping a healthy breakfast is counterproductive because you need fuel to energize yourself, and a good breakfast also makes you less prone to overeat later in the day. If you schedule twenty minutes of exercise each morning, too, you'll double

your energy boost, which will carry you through the rough spots and help you to stay focused.

2. **Follow the "Rule of Two."** My trademarked Rule of Two involves spending five minutes each morning writing a list of the day's tasks, circling the two most important tasks, and focusing only on those two tasks. If you approach each day faced with five or even thirty tasks, you'll feel paralyzed by the sheer workload ahead. Instead, ask yourself, what are the two most crucial tasks for today that I should take care of, if I do nothing else? Focus only on those two tasks. When they are completed, focus on the next two most essential tasks. If you organize your day by your most important priorities, you'll celebrate real accomplishments at the end of the day. (For more Rule of Two tips, visit www.ruthklein.com.)

3. **Post your plan on a calendar.** Before you head off for work, write your schedule on a large calendar to post in the most visible place in your home or office. This allows you to visualize and focus on your daily and weekly schedule without losing track of your priorities.

4. **Take control of your e-mail.** The 24/7 availability of e-mail doesn't mean you should waste several hours a day continually checking your e-mail or BlackBerry messages. First, don't immediately check your e-mail in the morning. Second, schedule only three or four times a day when you will pick up your e-mail. Third, strive to respond to multiple e-mails from the same person with one e-mailed reply summarizing your responses. It's a smart way to avoid e-mail traffic jams at the start of your workday and throughout the work week. You can adapt a similar schedule for taking control of when and how often you check your phone and PDA messages.

5. **Organize and systemize.** Dealing with those mounds of paper that greet you each morning can take fewer than ten or twenty minutes each day if you organize and systemize. Divide everything into categories (work, home, school, projects, tasks, invitations, bills). Create color-coded files for each category. Attach a note with a paper clip to each file in your "system," indicating the dates that responses or actions are due. Once you get into the habit of spending a few minutes a day filing papers, you'll feel in control and will avoid missing deadlines or wasting time searching through piles of paperwork for the document you need. Spending

a few minutes organizing and categorizing papers each morning (if you are a high-energy afternoon or evening person; instead, do it after lunch or before leaving work if you're a high-energy morning person) will save you several hours each week.

How to Take a One-Minute Vacation

At mid-morning, take a one-minute vacation. Spend one minute at the "gym" by taking a healthy walk outdoors or through the hallways. Spend one minute at the spa by practicing deep breathing exercises. Inhale slowly, and then exhale slowly to bring energizing oxygen to your brain and body and to relax tense muscles. Spend one minute on an island or any other destination that you can daydream about. Shut your eyes and imagine yourself at your favorite place, and relax your breathing and your muscles as you daydream. Momentarily shifting your mental focus away from a stressful problem will allow you time to relax and then refocus.

Sit Up!

Spending long hours sitting at a computer can create an enormous strain on your body. Physicians advise that you take frequent breaks throughout the day and also pause to stretch. Even the chair at your desk can trigger stress. Office supply stores now carry more brands of ergonomically correct chairs than ever before. They are more expensive than poorly made chairs are, but weigh that price tag against the high cost of a doctor's visit. Sitting correctly can also prevent exhaustion and tired muscles. The American Chiropractic Association recommends that you position yourself so that there are two inches between the front edge of your seat and the back of your knees. For more good posture tips, visit the association's Web site at www.amerchiro.org.

Take Five to Seven Minutes Every Morning at Work

Take five to seven minutes every morning to get grounded for the day. Do not make or receive any phone calls, attend any meetings, or start any projects for the first five to seven minutes.

The quiet time you spend will help you to focus positively on the day ahead, and higher productivity and calmness will result.

You may also find this five- to seven-minute grounding period helpful at other times during the day.

daily aspiration   "I am a powerful beam of light."

21 take control of the phone

Today's technology leaves you feeling as if your ears are always ringing, when it's actually your telephone, cell phone, and PDA. With access to so many communication devices, you now have the opportunity to feel overwhelmed twenty-four hours a day. You also have the ability to spread your stress dis-ease to others by contributing to the overuse of telephones and cell phones. You can reduce the time you spend on your phone and downsize your stress levels by following these easy steps to make a phone schedule and stick to it, respond to people the correct way, and follow the rules of good phone manners.

Count the number of calls you accept during your workday for a week, then multiply this by five (assuming your phone calls will only last five minutes). This will give you a very low estimate of the time you have spent on the phone that day.

dear diva

"I get interrupted by phone calls all day long, but I have to answer my phone. How can I handle the constant interruptions?"

secrets from the de-stress diva

First of all, do you really have to answer every call as it comes in? Really? I would say that you don't have to. I have heard so many reasons why people feel that they have to take each call as it comes in. Think about it. What did you do before cell phones were invented, when you were away from your office phone? Chances are, you were inundated then as well. Now, add an additional twenty-five calls per day during all hours of the day, and it's no wonder that you're crazed and stressed out because of the phone. If you would like to download a free report called *No Zone Cell Phone*, please go to www.ruthklein. com/nzcp. It gives advice on cell phone etiquette.

Here are some other tips to help you be in control of your phone, rather than your phone controlling you and your time:

- **Cluster phone messages.** Check your voice mail only three to four times daily, and return your messages three to four times a day. This is enough response time to return calls in most industries. You can check and return calls every two hours or so.

- **Turn off your cell phone.** Keep your cell phone off or on "silent" during most of the day. Otherwise, you will be interrupted constantly, and you'll lose hours of precious time.

- **Keep the caller I.D. out of sight.** Make sure you can't see the caller I.D. on your cell phone or land line so that you're not tempted to take the call while you're working.

- **Don't put your cell phone on the table.** Keep your cell phone off any table where you eat, which includes coffee houses. In addition to being rude, having your cell phone in plain sight doesn't allow you to relax while you're eating and digesting food.

> daily aspiration   "I am effortlessly in control of my phone."

22 e-mail: when you reach the limit

E-mail overload is slowing our ability to manage time at home and on the job. The daily barrage of hundreds of bits of information is becoming a stress trigger in its own right. In a 2005 study for Hewlett-Packard, the University of London reported that 62 percent of workers are addicted to checking their e-mail even at home or on vacation. Half of those surveyed reported the habit of immediately responding to e-mails, even when doing so interrupted a meeting. More important, the same eye-opening study found that a workers' functioning IQs drops measurably when they are constantly distracted by phone calls and e-mails.

dear diva

"I have so much e-mail in my inbox that I can't get my regular work done. I can't get it under control. How often should I check my e-mail without becoming overstressed?"

secrets from the de-stress diva

You can't control all spam, and you can't control how many times a day you receive legitimate e-mails, either. What you can control is the time you spend responding to and answering your e-mail, which is a smart way to de-stress your inbox and outbox.

- **Do not check your e-mail when you first wake up.** Unless you're a physician or an emergency worker, checking your e-mail when you first wake up only serves to create stress at the start of your day and takes you completely off course for what you need to do for the day.

- **Do not check your e-mail for the first hour to two hours of your workday.** Most of us check our e-mail the moment we get into the office out of habit, not because it makes our day more productive. In fact, the opposite occurs. When you check your e-mail first thing after getting to the office, chances are good that this one habit will contribute to a loss of at least an hour for the day. Start your workday with the two most important tasks for the day and then, one to two hours after you have started your workday, go ahead and check your e-mail.

- **Check your e-mail only at scheduled times of the day.** Depending on the nature of your work, check your e-mail only two or three times a day. I check my e-mail three times on most days—10 A.M., 1 P.M., and 4 P.M.—and only occasionally in the evenings if I am involved in a project that requires working at night, which I keep to a minimum.

- **Let others know that you check your e-mail only at certain times of the day.** Continually checking our e-mail has become so habitual that others expect us to immediately respond, too, when an e-mail is sent. When other people know that you check your e-mail only at certain times, they will not anticipate an immediate answer. If it's an emergency, tell them to call you instead. The bonus is that others will pick up the idea and try it themselves, which will go far toward unclogging your inbox.

- **Wait before you respond.** If you receive several e-mails a day with different requests from the same person, wait to respond. Then, respond with one e-mail containing the responses to every question. Other people may get into the habit of sending fewer and more all-inclusive e-mails, too, when they see you doing it.

- **Use your best e-mail manners.** The very nature of e-mail can make good e-mail etiquette essential to prevent someone from misinterpreting your brief messages. (Is it too harsh? Are you capitalizing every letter, which in the language of e-mail amounts to shouting?) Reread your message before you send it to ensure that it is clear and politely worded. Include a "please" or a "thank you." Did you know that courtesy is contagious, too?

- **Divide and conquer.** Create a different e-mail address for important personal correspondence or for e-newsletters. You can't eliminate spam entirely, but having different addresses can prevent the loss of important messages. Keep a separate e-mail account for important personal correspondence, in addition to your main e-mail box. Creating a separate e-mail address for e-newsletters and other general accounts helps to divert to this address the mountains of spam that tend to accompany such subscriptions.

- **Don't let spam filters block important information.** In the unsuccessful efforts to eliminate unwanted e-mails, today's spam blockers often toss out the good with the bad, causing workers to become stressed over lost e-mails. Check your spam folder once a day to ensure that you have not missed any important messages.

Avoid Computer Eye Strain

The American Optometric Association reported that computer vision syndrome (CVS) affects almost 90 percent of the millions of Americans who work on computers every day. According to the association, symptoms of CVS include dry eyes, eyestrain, light sensitivity, neck and/or backaches and fatigue. Your computer-tired eyes can also produce headaches, blurred vision, and neck and shoulder aches and pains. To avoid computer eyestrain, optometrists recommend that every few minutes you spend several seconds looking away from your screen at an object located at least five to ten feet away from your computer. Look in one direction, then in another, and finally return your attention to the computer screen.

One-Minute Meditation

1. Inhale slowly, while mentally counting to 1.
2. Exhale, and inhale again, mentally counting to 2, and then exhale.
3. Repeat until you've counted to 10.

Calming with Light

Take a five-minute break from your computer, and calmly focus on lit candles, fresh flowers, and a daily aspiration for the day.

> daily aspiration   "I work effortlessly and calmly with my incoming e-mail."

23 where did the time go?

The Society for Human Resource Management called it "work intensification" and added that it's one of the top trends in the workplace. It's all about employers trying to squeeze more productivity from fewer employees and is a major cause of workplace stress. A survey by the global management consulting firm Accenture confirmed that nearly two-thirds of employees reported an increased workload. Thus, time-management skills become crucial in how you establish your priorities and schedules to meet higher workplace demands and eliminate the "time wasters" in your workday to keep modern stress at bay. This advice also applies to professionals, the self-employed, and management ranks.

dear diva

"I never seem to have enough time to do it all at work or at home. I need help!"

secrets from the de-stress diva

Time management is really life management. How you spend your days either moves you closer to or farther away from your goals and dreams. Your ability to focus your time and energy on high-value priorities helps determine in large part the amount of joy or stress you experience daily.

Try this exercise, even though it is time-consuming. Create a daily time sheet and make seven copies. For the next seven days, write down how you are spending your day at each thirty-minute interval. After one week, you will have discovered how much time you are wasting, instead of being productive. You'll find yourself eliminating those time-wasters in the future.

Go to my Web site to download a daily time sheet: www.ruthklein.com/dailytime.

- **Drive and learn.** Turn driving time into learning time, and listen to CDs or audiocassettes in your car. The average driver, according to the American Automobile Association, drives 12,000 to 25,000 miles each year, which amounts to twenty-five forty-hour weeks and equals two full university semesters spent behind the wheel of his or her car each year.

- **Just do it.** Yes, the makers of Nike shoes had it right when their advertisements urged, "Just do it." Too much time can be spent on planning, rather than on actually accomplishing the task. Procrastination is also the result when you worry that you might not do the task perfectly. The fear of failure can paralyze you. Don't strive for perfection, strive to get the job done right. This important change in mind-set will help you better manage your time at work and at home. While you make the "perfect" proposal, cake, decorations, or whatever else you think needs to be perfect, you lose out on opportunities that you never see because you are so obsessed with doing something perfectly. Plus, trying to achieve perfection is a huge waste of time. I find that a lot of procrastination occurs because people spend so much time and effort trying to make something perfect. Just do it. Once you have started the task or the project, work to the best of your experience and expertise and then finish it. You can always course-correct.

- **Remain unattached to the outcome.** Do the best you can in whatever you're doing, whether it is working on a project or working on a relationship. You can have an intention of what you would like the result to be. Once you have created the intention, however, you need to let go. When you can live in the present and not be attached to the outcome, your stress level will immediately go down.

- **Prioritize.** Create a list of your immediate goals, and set your priorities according to whether these will help you meet your ultimate career and lifestyle goals. If the tasks you are performing do not relate to meeting your main goals, begin to eliminate them or dramatically reduce the time you spend on those tasks. Circle the high-priority tasks and devote more attention to them.

- **Organize.** Every morning, create a to-do list that places your two most important priorities at the top. As you complete the first and then the second priority, circle the next two priorities and accomplish them. You will find that this system helps you stay present as new priorities shift during the day.

- **Delegate.** Delegate tasks that are not vital to meeting your personal goals. Delegate household chores to household members. Delegate work that is not important today to another time or day.

- **Simplify.** Clutter can create havoc with your time-management goals. Eliminate nonessentials on your desk and in your home. Spend at least ten minutes each day sorting and filing (using a simple filing system) important papers and tossing the rest. Remove all items from the center of your desk that are not essential to your top-priority task. This will keep you focused on, and only on, the immediate priority.

- **Make your health and happiness a priority.** You will better manage your time at work and at home if you manage your health and happiness in order to energize and inspire yourself to meet your goals. On your daily to-do list, add time for exercise, healthy eating, and an enjoyable activity. It will make an enormous difference in how you respond to daily stresses.

Easy Five-Minute Meditation

Meditation will help you to slow down and refocus on the task at hand. In a recent University of Pennsylvania study, a group of seventeen beginners showed great improvement in their focus after meditating for a half-hour five times a week for eight weeks. Meditation also increased their ability to manage tasks while staying alert at work. Find a quiet area and focus only on following your breath. When other thoughts come to mind, just say, "Thank you," let them pass, and go right back to focusing on your breathing. Do this for five minutes three to four times a day, and watch your stress levels go down while your concentration improves. The trick, however, is to do it daily.

Time-Saving Elder Care Resources

As life spans continue to increase, many people are facing new demands on their time as they begin to take care of elder parents part- or full-time. Here are some resources to help you find answers to your questions and, hopefully, to de-stress you and your family:

AARP (www.aarp.org/families/caregiving) will advise you on the logistics of setting up long-term care.

The Administration on Aging (www.aoa.gov) is a government site that is part of the Department of Health and Human Services.

Family Caregiver Alliance (www.caregiver.org) is a great site for elder-care resources, organizations, and fact sheets.

CaringBridge (www.caringbridge.org) helps families set up a free Web site so that everyone can stay connected.

Lotsa Helping Hands (www.lotsahelpinghands.com) helps families coordinate the tasks that are required in elder care.

Make a Clear Request and Follow Up

You may often find that you are "left holding the bag" in regard to taking on the responsibilities of others. This uses up a great deal of time and also increases your stress levels. Rather than merely letting people dump work or projects in your lap, especially if they have mentioned earlier that they will help do the work, here is a way that you can clear up the confusion, lower your stress level, and create more time for activities that are high on your priority list:

Make a clear request of what you want or need and then follow up.

Here are a couple of examples:

"I have a list of tasks to do right now. Where is this on the priority list of the ten other items you have given me?" It makes the other person prioritize instead of merely dumping projects on your desk, and the individual is able to see the amount of work and time that is necessary for each.

"It was my understanding that you were going to take care of this. I am doing these three items for the event, and I need you to follow up on these other items."

Triplicate Effect

Most of the negative stress in our lives can be traced to poor time management. We become frantic because we believe that we don't have enough hours in the day to accomplish all of our tasks. The Triplicate Effect is my trademarked method of maximizing your day the stress-free way and helping you accomplish all of your tasks.

Here's how it works. Think in triplicate when you work on a project, go on a business trip, write an article, make a healthy meal, reply to an e-mail, host an event, or undertake other tasks. What can you accomplish with the same information or ingredients to produce three valuable results? When I am in my office writing an article, I prepare it with the Triplicate Effect in mind. When I finish my article for a magazine, I immediately revise it to fit the style and the needs of my newsletter and also place it in my schedule as a topic for my national *Time Management Secrets* radio show. Sometimes, I'll double the Triplicate Effect by using the same information as a basis for my blog, as a topic for an upcoming television interview, and also as information for a sales letter to potential business clients. I don't have to reinvent the wheel, so I save time and stress using the Triplicate Effect.

Four More Ways to Apply the Triplicate Effect to a Task

- **Writing a one-page announcement about your product or service** . . . becomes a news release (Just add who, what, when, where, and why) . . . and then becomes the basis for an article for your blog or for a local newspaper . . . and finally becomes a highlighted selling point in your next sales letter to a client.
- **Hard-boiling eggs to refrigerate for later** . . . becomes a high-protein evening snack . . . and then becomes a quick breakfast for you and your children with toast and juice . . . and finally becomes the main ingredient in an egg salad sandwich for your lunch.
- **Buying several shoebox-sized plastic boxes to store your kitchen wares** . . . then becomes a new way to store vitamins and medications under your bathroom counter . . . and also becomes an under-the-desk holder of extra pens and other supplies in your office . . . and finally becomes a storage bin for photographs that will be sorted and placed in an album later.
- **Taking a child or a parent to the doctor's office** . . . becomes an opportunity to drop off dry cleaning or paperwork on the way . . . and also becomes an opportunity to spend valuable time with a loved one, engaging in a supportive conversation . . . and finally becomes an opportunity to check your cell phone messages and take notes while you're seated in the waiting room.

Once you master the Triplicate Effect, you'll find yourself running errands, cooking, shopping, writing reports, making phone calls, going on business trips, planning family events, and doing myriad other tasks in a way that will maximize your valuable time by producing at least three profitable results. Isn't that so much less stressful?

Focus on Actions, not on Results

Success is not measured by results because you cannot always control the results of your actions. Rather, success means using your personal abilities to perform at your best. This requires knowing the goal, choosing the wisest course of action, and taking pride in doing your utmost to carry it out. Following these steps will always result in the optimal and most sustainable outcome that you are capable of achieving.

> daily aspiration   "I have enough time to do what I need to do today effortlessly."

24 beginning those hard-to-start projects

You know the feeling. For one reason or another, you just can't begin a certain project. You think it will be unpleasant, too challenging, or even stressful, and you wind up adding to your stress by putting it off until other pressures force you to start. Sometimes you find to your surprise that the task was easy and you were making a monster out of a pussycat. But other times you end up facing an urgent deadline. Stress builds and you scurry to complete the project without giving it your best. You can feel further stress afterward, worrying about the consequences. Hard-to-start projects are usually the ones you need to begin early. There's no reason to feel any stress at all from a simple task, and it is equally futile to feel the dire, oppressive stress that results from postponing a hard one.

dear diva

"It's difficult getting started on a project I have been postponing. How can I motivate myself to begin?"

secrets from the de-stress diva

Look at your calendar, and write or type in when you would like to start working on the project. Reschedule any meetings, if possible, and enforce a "quiet zone" from phone calls. Put your phones on voice mail, and *do not* answer the phone for one hour. Unless it's an emergency—and there are very few real ones, thank goodness—no one will suffer.

Then *just start*. You may often find yourself not wanting to do something because you don't know where to begin. Once you start, however, you've solved that problem. And you usually find yourself becoming involved in the project as you go along. Again, if you don't know where to start, *just start*.

Stay present and focus on the project. Begin the project, and time yourself for thirty minutes. After you start the project, chances are good that you will stay with it for a longer period. When doubt arises in your mind, gently let it go. If you find that you need more information, do what is necessary to find it or, if possible, delegate the information-gathering process to someone else.

The first time is usually the toughest. If, however, you find that it's difficult to start each time you work on this project, take five minutes to randomly write what you're feeling and thinking at the moment. What kinds of projects do you tend to put off? Answer as honestly as you can. This little bit of information will give you loads of insight as to *why* you're having such a difficult time working on this project, and at the very least, it will help you to "dump" and let go of anxiety.

Aromatherapy

Peppermint oil is good for mental focus and clarity, while basil oil helps stimulate memory. Place one or two drops on a handkerchief and sniff.

Bach Flower Essence

Hornbeam fights that "Monday morning" feeling. This flower essence helps to refresh your energy and motivates you to face the day's work.

Yoga

To help restore circulation and alleviate anxiety:

1. Place both of your thumbs in the middle of your forehead. Make small circles by rubbing your forehead with your thumbs.
2. Move your fingers across your brow toward your temples. Pause there and massage. This is an area where you hold stress and tension.
3. Take a deep breath. Open your mouth and your eyes wide and stick out your tongue as far as it will go. Say, "Aaaghhhh," and look up as you exhale forcefully. Repeat three times.

> daily aspiration   "I have enough time to start my new project."

25 now, where is that important document?

Organization is a powerful weapon to use against stress on the job, and it begins with your desk. A survey of managers by the office label–making company DYMO found that more than half of employers equate an employee's organizational skills with job performance. A messy desk is a bottom-line factor for employers. According to the same study, it is estimated that every misplaced piece of paperwork costs a company $120, as reported by *USA Today*. Applying smart organizational skills to de-clutter your office can take only a few minutes a day, and you'll reap the long-term rewards.

dear diva

"I spend too many hours looking for important documents because my office is so cluttered. I can't seem to make enough time to clear it out or organize my workspace, even though my boss and clients have commented negatively on the appearance of my office. How can I create an office that's clean and organized?"

secrets from the de-stress diva

1. **Assess space opportunities.** Do you have a closet or a bookcase that can be used to store nonpriority files, extra office supplies, and background reports? Do you have space outside your office to store items that you will not need today, this week, or this month? If so, use that space to store things that you do not need immediately.

2. **Take immediate steps to de-clutter.** Each day, resolve to remove one unnecessary item from your office.

3. **End your week with a ten-minute purge.** Spend ten minutes before the end of your workweek purging excess paperwork or old files. This will get rid of clutter clusters that are impossible to clear out on a daily basis, without causing you too much stress or wasting a lot of time.

4. **Organize and systemize.** Organize paperwork, reports, and other documents into folders that are filed by a system of priorities. Place your top-priority files at the front, and move them to the back when they are completed. Immediately file incoming materials into your organized files, or place them in the center of your desk if they are identified as immediate priorities.

5. **Remove excess personal clutter.** Minimize or entirely remove your stock of personal photos and mementos.

6. **De-clutter your computer.** Organize your desktop files into computer file folders that are easily marked to help you move desktop files into those folders at the end of each workday.

7. **Clear walkways and floor space.** This will create a perception of more space, while also removing obstacles that you, your employers or staff, or important guests might trip over.

8. **Don't become a dumping ground.** If you are participating in a joint project, appoint a team member to become the central filing and paperwork resource. If a coworker wants to leave a stack of papers for you to review, offer instead to visit your coworker's office to review them there. This also presents an opportunity for you to take a break away from your office.

9. **Learn from others.** Visit other de-cluttered offices to pick up tips on how to best de-clutter your workspace.

10. **Clean workspaces.** Wipe down or dust shelves and desktops. Keep your computer clean by using cleaning products that are especially designed for computer stations, keyboards, and other technology devices. Empty trash bins daily. Do not keep food items in your office that will create unpleasant smells. Keep a moisturizing hand sanitizer inside a desk drawer to kill germs while you remove ink from your hands that has rubbed off reports.

Clearing Off Your Desk

Clearing off your desk will reflect your priorities, while also shaving hours off your week that you would have spent diving through the mess to find important files and papers.

- Clear off the top of your desk. It should contain only your most important projects and files. Place them in the center of your desk.

- Use the space beneath your desk to keep files you will soon need but don't need now. Stack mail or memos that can be read later. Stash a bottle of water under your desk to keep yourself hydrated.

- Organize your desk drawers so that each holds one systemized filing system. For example, use one drawer for files you will use this week, another for background files, another drawer for office supplies, and one drawer to keep desktop supplies such as pens, ink cartridges, paper clips, and staplers.

- Keep your trash at bay. Use only a small trash can to get yourself into the habit of emptying it often throughout the day, thus minimizing the look of too much clutter.
- Clear your desk before you leave for work each day, leaving only your top two projects in the center of your desk. This will immediately focus your attention on your priorities when you arrive the next day.

> daily aspiration
>
> "I am enjoying a clean, organized office."

26 your peak energy pick-me-up

Today's employees are working longer hours than ever, with the traditional workweek now stretching to fifty or sixty hours and upward. At the same time, a recent study at the University of California at Irvine reported a direct correlation between the stress of longer workweeks and high blood pressure and other serious illnesses. Long hours can be dangerous to your health. Again, smart time-management skills can help you to focus on your toughest assignments during your Peak Energy hours. This allows you extra time during the rest of the day to wind down and be proactive about planning and organizing your schedule for the next day at work. Most people have their Peak Energy hours in the morning, but there are many others who have them at different times during the day.

dear diva

"There is so much work to do, by the middle of the afternoon I feel overstressed and drained of the energy I need to finish the day. I am so overwhelmed, it's hard to even picture going home to face more responsibilities. How can I end my day on a productive note, instead of feeling stressed and exhausted?"

secrets from the de-stress diva

1. **Know your Peak Energy time.** Every person has a different internal rhythm that makes him or her feel "at a peak" at certain times of the day but not at others. Some of us are morning people, some of us are mid-morning people, some are mid-afternoon people, and others feel most energetic in the evening. Knowing your Peak Energy time will allow you to concentrate on your most important challenges at that time of the day.

2. **Use your Peak Energy time.** If you are an early-morning person, use your Peak Energy time to meet deadlines, which will allow you to focus on more mundane tasks in the afternoon. If you are an afternoon person, spend your mornings filing, scheduling, and planning your high-energy afternoon hours.

3. **Protect your Peak Energy time.** Learn to avoid scheduling meetings or other distracting tasks during your Peak Energy times. Let coworkers know that you will be unavailable during key hours of the day because that is when you focus on your most important projects. You can't avoid all distractions, but, whenever possible, learn to take control of and protect your Peak Energy times to minimize stress and maximize your productivity.

4. **Take an energizing afternoon break.** Schedule an energizing afternoon break every day to relax, exercise, refresh, and refocus on your priorities. Simply stop what you are doing, and take a walk up and down the stairs or outside the building. If you can't leave, do stretching exercises at your desk. Instead of a cup of coffee, take deep breaths as you walk or stretch, to carry energizing oxygen to your brain and muscles. Take a walk around your office while you return phone calls.

5. **Visualize a stopping point; then stop.** Afternoons will be less stressful if you visualize a stopping point. At mid-afternoon, take five minutes to assess your progress. Then simplify. Visualize finishing one project by the end of the workday, rather than trying to juggle six half-done projects that will leave you feeling frustrated when you stop working. Example: It's 2 P.M., and you have three projects on your desk. Choose the one you most likely can complete (or a piece of the project you can complete) by 5 P.M. Visualize completing this project, then move forward. By the end

of the day, you will have completed a task that will leave you feeling that you've done your best, instead of feeling overwhelmed.

6. **Plan ahead for the next day.** Ten minutes before you stop working, take five minutes to organize your desk and another five minutes to write down your top two priorities for the next morning. This habit will leave you feeling in control and will give you a stress-free head start for the next morning.

7. **Plan ahead for your evenings.** Anticipating stress at home will make you feel anxious before you leave the office. Instead, visualize and then erase obstacles to a stress-free, relaxing, and reenergizing evening away from work. If the thought of cooking a large dinner makes you feel overwhelmed, erase the obstacle by visualizing an easy, healthy meal and then resolving to prepare a simple meal.

If you feel anxious about household chores or social obligations awaiting your arrival, visualize and then erase the obstacle. Immediately delegate household chores to other family members or to another day. Visualize and then erase too many social obligations by saying yes to only one a week or even one every two weeks. Celebrate the extra time you'll have by visualizing yourself relaxed and enjoying your stress-free evening.

On the Refreshing Power of Meditation

Meditation in the workplace is a growing trend that is benefiting overworked employees and managers who often lose focus midway through the workday. According to the Society for Human Resource Management, more than 60 percent of companies now offer wellness programs, up from 53 percent in 2001, and one-third of workplaces provide acupuncture or coverage for this treatment, up from 18 percent five years ago. Several companies hold meditation classes. There are numerous ways to meditate, whether in a classroom setting, alone at your desk, or outdoors.

Here's a simple Buddhist technique, credited to C. George Boeree of Shippensburg University, that you can do at your desk or during an afternoon break.

1. Sit or kneel in a comfortable position.

2. Gently shake your hands until they feel loose. Turn your palms up and rest your hands on top of each other, gently.
3. Close your eyes or focus on a nearby object as you hold your head erect.
4. Breathe deeply, then slowly exhale, counting to as high as 10 while you exhale. Repeat this process and continue for ten to fifteen minutes.

> daily aspiration
>
> "I am calm and focused this afternoon at work."

27 the short and sweet meeting

Even in today's high-stress, long-hours workplace, researchers report that traditional meetings still dominate at most companies. Meetings can stretch into hours in length, creating more stress to already time-strapped employees who must dedicate time away from their tasks for traditionally organized meetings.

Smart workplaces feature shorter "action meetings," at which agendas zero in on the most important issues and limit presentations to strict time periods. Even if you are not in a position to control a meeting agenda, you can keep your contributions brief, relying on handouts if that saves you time. Not every meeting has to address every issue. More companies are also turning to mini-meetings, which involve only the key people who are working together on a project.

dear diva

"I hate meetings because they waste my time, they waste everybody else's time, and they are usually led by people who just like to hear themselves talk. If I have to have a meeting or get up and speak at one, I feel that much more stressed. How can I make meetings less stressful?"

secrets from the de-stress diva

Meetings are a way of life in the workplace. Whether you are the one who leads or you attend the meeting as a participant, however, there are five things you can do to de-stress meetings:

1. **Have your meetings in the afternoon.** Why? Because most people have high energy in the mornings, and this is when the most productive work that requires planning and concentration occurs.

2. **Keep meetings to fifty minutes or less,** unless it's a brainstorming session.

3. **Send out an agenda** to everyone before the meeting and ask for anything that they would like to add. This way, there are no surprises in the meeting, and people have an idea of what is coming up so they can mentally prepare for the meeting.

4. **Accountability** at each meeting is an integral part of moving forward and building on each time everyone meets. Decide who is responsible for what during the meeting, and make sure this is written in the minutes.

5. **Follow up** on things that have been delegated during each meeting. This one tip will save you time, frustration, and money.

Here are some other ideas to de-stress meetings:

1. **Don't meet.** Seriously, ask yourself whether a meeting with everyone in the office is necessary to announce a new policy that can be summarized on paper or in an e-mail and disseminated. Do fifty people need to attend a meeting, when only five key people are required to be there? If you can't think of a measurably important reason to have a meeting, don't schedule one.

2. **Schedule only smart meetings.** Don't schedule meetings just to say you've had them. Is there a problem that can be solved only with a meeting? Are there three problems that can be solved only with a meeting? If so, make those three problems your agenda, and distribute the agenda well in advance of the meeting. This will allow everyone involved to have ample time to prepare solutions.

3. **Set time limits and stick to them.** Think back to your school days, when you found yourself daydreaming or dreaming up mischief forty-five minutes into an hour-long class. Keep your meetings short and to the point. If you say that you will end your meeting in thirty minutes, do it. If you did not meet your goals within that

time, study what happened to ensure that your next meeting will be more productive.

4. **Allow no distractions.** Mandate that all cell phones, laptops, and other electronic devices be turned off. This will force participants to focus on the meeting without distractions.

5. **Create an escape hatch.** Your follow-up plan is your escape hatch. Announce at the start of your meeting that issues left unresolved or remaining questions can be addressed by a five-minute follow-up meeting involving only interested parties, an e-mail exchange, or a telephone call. Announcing your follow-up plan at the start of the meeting will help you end all meetings on time.

6. **Be prepared.** Whether you are giving or going to a meeting, be prepared with answers to questions or problems that will be addressed. If you don't know what will be addressed, ask well in advance. Take good notes during the meeting to be ready immediately afterward with any follow-up questions.

7. **Be flexible.** If you find yourself at a long meeting that deals with one problem or issue, be flexible enough to use that time well. Even if you already know the answer to a problem, consider the extra time you are forced to spend in a meeting to be time you can use to look at the problem from other perspectives, instead of only one. Write the pros and cons of each approach on paper. It may further fine-tune your approach in considering this and future topics.

Smart Help with Meetings

Dozens of Web sites provide step-by-step help in planning effective meetings, on topics that range from facilitating a meeting to creating a practical agenda. For free starters, visit the "meetings" feature at www.freegeek.com or go to www.meetingwizard.org.

Addressing Meetings

If you are worried about standing up and speaking in front of a group, the rule of thumb is to keep it short. People who are uncomfortable about speaking in front of groups will only add to their stress if they prepare long talks. A smart way to do this is to limit your opening comments to one or two sentences, then tell the group that you have three questions (or two or six) that you want answered at the meeting, and say that you will dedicate your time in front of them to simply asking the questions.

Ask the first question. When someone responds, give that person adequate time to answer. Ask whether there are any comments. Then, ask the question again to learn whether anyone else can contribute. (Again, ask for comments after each question has been answered.) Have someone in the group volunteer to take notes on the answers. End your meeting after you have asked and received answers to your questions. If you run out of time, request that meeting participants answer your questions by e-mail or by scheduling a conversation with you later, outside of the meeting.

You don't need jokes, anecdotes, guest speakers, slide shows, or PowerPoint demonstrations. Just ask your questions and request answers. And limit your Q&A to a set time. It's that simple.

> daily aspiration   "I will stay present at meetings and help to keep them short and useful."

28 compromise and cooperation: they really work

De-stressing your life at work, with friends, or at home involves learning the art of compromise and cooperation. The Counseling and Mental Health Center at the University of Texas at Austin suggests, "Consider a disagreement or unmet need through the other party's eyes. From that vantage, is a compromise possible?"

"I can't seem to get my coworkers at the office or my children at home to cooperate, especially on days when I face stressful deadlines. I wish I knew the secret to avoiding confrontations that make me angry instead of productive. How can I master the art of compromise?"

secrets from the de-stress diva

The University of Iowa Extension Services found effective lessons in compromise and cooperation in a report based on the book *Managing Conflicts on the Farm*, by Guy Hutt and Robert Milligan. The lessons are useful for city dwellers, too. Conflict creates stress and inhibits productivity; only compromise and cooperation allow us to replace conflicts with positive actions.

1. **Invite compromise.** Ask everyone involved in a dispute to openly address a conflict in one place.
2. **Establish a common goal.** Even if everyone disagrees on how a project should be accomplished, establish a common goal. Is the common goal getting a project done on time or planning a family event that will not involve stress? Begin with establishing common goals, which will lay the foundation for finding a compromise.
3. **Listen.** Listen, and write down summaries of the diverse viewpoints that are expressed about how to reach a common goal.
4. **Mediate.** Ask a volunteer or an outsider to gather information about the diverse viewpoints and to recommend a compromise.
5. **Negotiate cooperation.** Ask everyone at the table to be willing to cooperate to reach a goal. Inviting the active participation of all involved in the issue allows people to share in a solution, versus choosing one person's solutions over another's, and thus it eliminates conflict.

Identify Your Commonalities

Identify as many common goals and values at the outset, or even as you get involved in the process, of a meeting or a problem with differing and resistant viewpoints. This is an excellent way to discover that you may have more in common than you first thought. Here is an easy and valuable exercise you can use to identify commonalities. On a piece of paper, create a column for each party involved in the negotiation or collaborative exercise. List each person's goals, values, and viewpoints regarding the issue you are discussing. Then identify the common ground among all parties.

Stay Calm

One of the most effective strategies to keep your stress level down and stay alert and in a problem-solving mode is to keep calm. Here are two suggestions for how to stay calm in the middle of a very stressful situation:

1. Breathe slowly and deeply.
2. Slowly count to 10 forward and then again backward.
3. Create an "internal agenda" of fairness and moving the discussion forward.
4. Stay unattached to the outcome: whatever happens, know that this is the way it needs to be for now. Being attached to the outcome, especially if it is not what you wanted, will dramatically increase your stress levels.

> daily aspiration "I am cooperative in my work and personal dealings, and I have no attachment to them today."

29 de-stress with employees

A study by the Anxiety Disorders Association of America found that overwhelmed workers are often not willing to discuss workplace stress with managers. Only 40 percent of employees suffering from stress have raised the subject with employers; they list reasons that range from fear of repercussions to worries about being labeled ineffective or "weak." Of those who did speak to their employees, the study found that only 40 percent were offered help from their employers. Thus, it falls upon the employer to recognize and respond to symptoms of stress in the workplace. Otherwise, employers risk a loss of productivity, greater medical costs, higher job turnover, and other increased costs to the corporate bottom line. In a recent study, the U.S. Occupational Safety and Health Administration found that stress is contagious; therefore, ignoring the ill effects of stress among employees will only make matters worse because this stress will spread throughout the workforce.

dear diva

"I can feel the tensions boiling outside my office door, and I sense that my workers are not listening to me or to one another. This is going to be a bottom-line problem if I don't deal with it now. What can I do as an employer to de-stress my employees?"

secrets from the de-stress diva

1. **Listen.** The simple act of listening will allow you to pinpoint who is feeling stress, at what level, on which projects, and on what days. Ask your employees what is causing them stress on the job, and listen.

2. **Act.** Ignoring stress will lead to bottom-line results, and not the positive kind. Employee turnover, lost productivity, and too many sick days from overstress are huge expenses. Ask yourself, will it ultimately be more costly to pile on the deadlines and the workload and suffer the high price of stress in today's workplace or to lighten up on the deadlines and the workload? Then, act accordingly.

3. **Bring in an expert.** Don't merely hire a consultant to create a report about a problem you already know exists. Find an expert on workplace stress who can productively address the problem in group and/or individual settings with your employees. In fact, consider asking an employee to work with you in lining up an outside stress expert.

4. **Lighten up.** Even if you don't have the budget to shower your workforce with raises or days off, you can lighten up so that your stress is not communicated to your workforce. If you feel stressed, don't address your employees until you have taken proactive steps to mitigate your own stress. Be generous with compliments for jobs well done. Give only constructive criticism.

5. **Anticipate glitches.** Workplace glitches come in the guise of pushed-up deadlines, technology malfunctions, and unexpected downturns. Expect them, and you can proactively plan ahead for how to weather them. Draw up a contingency plan now, before the next glitch.

6. **De-stress the workplace.** Ensure that the lighting is not too glaring and that your computers have well-placed screens and ergonomically correct seating. Mandate frequent breaks to allow your employees to de-stress, with frequent ten- or fifteen-minute periods throughout the day to return that personal phone call to their children, take an energizing walk, or just refocus on the task at hand. Do the same for yourself.

Yoga

This is a great yoga exercise to help relieve tension headaches, fatigue, and backaches.

1. Lay flat on your back with your arms outstretched at your sides in a 90-degree angle to your torso.
2. Inhale as you slowly bring both knees to your chest.
3. Roll both legs over to the right as you exhale, keeping your left shoulder on the ground as much as you can, while you turn your head in the opposite direction.
4. Hold the pose for two breathing cycles, and then roll your legs back to the center and over to the left, as you turn your head to the right.
5. Repeat this five or six times.

> daily aspiration "I empower my employees to be productive."

30 de-stress with colleagues

Ceridian LifeWorks, a provider of employee assistance programs, has collected dozens of examples of coworkers who spread tension among other staff members, increasing workplace stress. They range from colleagues with annoying personal habits, coworkers who abandon projects to their overstressed colleagues close to the deadline, and those who focus on unrelated topics right at the deadline, to those who throw tantrums or who don't say anything when disclosing information is vital. According to a recent report from *New Scientist*, the average worker wastes two hours each workday fielding e-mails, annoying colleagues, and phone calls.

dear diva

"I know five people at my job who drive me crazy on a daily basis. One asks too many questions. Another tells off-color jokes. Another one wants me to help him finish his work, while mine goes undone. I can't take this anymore. How can I avoid being distracted by annoying colleagues and still get my work done?"

secrets from the de-stress diva

Better communications is a key tool to improving relationships among colleagues, as is the emotional intelligence to respond in a way that minimizes the effect of a coworker's stress on your performance. Good manners have also proved to be a powerful weapon against stress caused by coworkers.

1. **Look in a mirror first.** When you notice yourself becoming annoyed at the way colleagues behave, take that important first step of looking in the mirror. Are you guilty of any of these behaviors? If so, take proactive steps to stop them.

2. **Identify and isolate.** Identify the people who are toxic to your productivity and isolate them. Stay away from areas of the workplace where they work and where they congregate. The goal is not to give them an opportunity to affect you.

3. **Don't procrastinate.** If a coworker is behaving badly, immediately confront the person and the situation before it becomes a long-term instigator of stress. Politely ask the coworker to stop a certain behavior and include a polite explanation. Examples: "I'm very busy in the mornings, so I keep my office quiet during these hours"; "I want to get this done well and efficiently, so I would appreciate your help in focusing on this deadline."

4. **Agree to disagree.** Respectfully agree to disagree with colleagues who insist that they are right. Example: "I agree that your work is important, although my deadline is my top priority right now." Example: "I respect your perspective, although I am going to proceed with . . ."

5. **Don't lose your temper.** Stress is contagious, and if an annoying colleague causes you to lose your temper, you, too, have become a source of stress in the workplace. When you see an irritating colleague approach and you can't leave the scene, immediately begin to breathe deeply and exhale slowly, to physically and emotionally calm yourself throughout the encounter and for five minutes after the encounter.

What If Your Coworker Has a Personality Disorder?

Psychologists Alan Cavaiola and Neil Lavender, in their book *Toxic Coworkers: How to Deal with Dysfunctional People on the Job,* describe colleagues with personality disorders as "a hidden cancer" in the workplace that can impact others' productivity and also their health. According to their research, people with personality disorders can view their symptoms as strengths, making it difficult for others to effectively confront them. The authors recommend avoiding these people whenever possible and, if you can't, to document their behavior in order to present a report to a superior.

Talk to Your Alter Ego

Close your eyes and imagine your alter ego sitting directly across from you. What question is your alter ego asking you? Answer all questions as honestly as you can. Listen to your alter ego's advice, if you trust it.

Eat Salad

Jill Nissenbaum, the Veggie Queen, suggests eating a salad with lots of greens (collards, spinach, kale, etc.) every day to lower your stress.

Aromatherapy

Certified phyto-aromatologist Kaliana Schmidt says that lemongrass has a purifying and an opening effect to clear up headaches and that "the electromagnetic field is shut down if the headache is caused by stress." She recommends that headache-sufferers use:

A 4-ounce misting bottle
distilled water
1 tablespoon Everclear liquor (180 proof)
5 drops lemongrass essential oil

Fill up the bottle with distilled water and the other two ingredients, and mist your face.

daily aspiration   "Today I will look for the gift each person has to offer me."

31 the impossible boss

The sitcom *The Office*, a popular British show with bad bosses as a major theme, was remade into an American version, which also proved to be a huge hit. The Internet abounds with e-newsletters and blogs featuring "worst boss" contests. Emotional intelligence can be a powerful tool to help you alleviate stress when dealing with bad-to-worse bosses in today's high-stress workplace.

dear diva

"My boss is a bully and piles on too many deadlines and work projects, then screams when his impossible deadlines aren't met. I hate going to work. How can I handle my impossible boss?"

secrets from the de-stress diva

Often, poor communications lead to a disconnect between what a boss expects from employees and what employees expect from the boss. Even self-employed people often fail to organize and prioritize in a way that focuses on achieving measurable goals.

1. **Use your emotional intelligence.** Your best weapon against a bad boss is your emotional intelligence. Learn what triggers his or her behavior and why, and act accordingly. If your boss is always in a bad mood on Monday, for example, avoid scheduling meetings with him or her on that day. If you can't avoid meetings, use your emotional intelligence to anticipate that your boss will behave badly on Mondays, and weather it until Tuesday.

2. **Refine your communication skills.** Study the communication strategies used by employees who are favored by your boss. Do they respond to questions with brief answers, or do they win praise by submitting detailed paper reports or e-mails? Follow suit. Watching and listening is a smart way to learn and use the communication strategies that are preferred by your boss.

3. **Create a daily performance report about yourself.** Be proactive. It's a great weapon against stress. At the end of each day, make a note of what progress you made on a report, what cost savings you produced, or other positive results. Think of it in terms of a line you would place on a mini-résumé, such as "Finished report two days early" and "Changed a procedure that saved the company xx dollars." Always have your mini-résumé ready when an overly critical boss asks just what it is you've been doing, anyway.

4. **Start looking.** Ask yourself whether working for an impossible boss is worth more than your life, because life-threatening stress is sabotaging many people in today's workplace. Numerous scientific studies link stress to high blood pressure, obesity, heart disease, and even cancer. Instead of responding with anger or feeling stressed,

focus your attention on networking, fine-tuning your résumé, and finding that next job with a great leader, not an impossible boss.

Stabilize Your Blood Sugar

Research has shown that eating five or six smaller meals throughout the day helps you cope with stress by lowering the stress hormone cortisol that is produced by the adrenal glands. It is said that these smaller meals regulate the feel-good hormones serotonin and dopamine.

Tai Chi

The Chinese have been doing tai chi for centuries. This is a great way to downshift by working with the body's energies through doing slow sequences of movements.

Drink Water

Water helps to flush toxins out of your body and keep you hydrated. Stress tends to dehydrate you. When you feel thirsty, you are already dehydrated to some extent.

The ABC Exercise

Elizabeth Andes-Bell, a yoga instructor, suggests the ABC Exercise: a ten-minute de-stressor to help you deal with a difficult situation at work.

Situation: Your boss yells at you and now you're in the bathroom fuming. Go through this process. Write down the following:

A. What happened. Just the facts (what the person did or said and what you did or said, not your interpretation of the facts).

B. What you believe. You interpret what has happened based on your beliefs.

C. What you feel. Your belief causes your feeling.

A triggers B. B triggers C. A *does not* cause B or C. You can change what you believe, and that change can trigger a different feeling.

Example:

A. Your boss yells at you.

B. You believe being yelled at means you are stupid and unworthy.

C. You experience feelings of shame and worthlessness.

Now rewrite A, B, and C so that your issues don't get triggered. Example:

A. Your boss yells at you

B. You realize people yell when they are overstressed and fearful.

C. You feel worthy and self-confident, because you did not take your boss's actions personally.

> daily aspiration   "I am a valuable employee."

32 saying "no" at work

Stress experts at the Mayo Clinic report that the stress that results from trying to squeeze in too many assignments at work, topped off by too many activities off the job, can be remedied with one word: *no*. According to the Mayo Clinic, the goal is to be honest with yourself and learn how to say no as a proactive deterrent against adding more stress to your job and life. "Saying no is not a selfish act," Mayo Clinic researchers stated in a recent report. "When you say no, you'll be able to spend quality time on the things you've already said yes to."

dear diva

"It seems like this always happens five minutes before the end of my day, when my superior walks in and asks whether I can help with a project that I know will take several more hours. Even though I'm exhausted, if I say no, I'm afraid I will not get a promotion or maybe I'll even lose my job. Everyone else is working long hours so I can't justify saying no, even though I feel stressed and angry about it. How do I say no without offending a colleague or placing my job in jeopardy?"

secrets from the de-stress diva

1. **Be honest with yourself.** Before you respond yes or no, learn to be honest with yourself. If you have time, write down the pros and cons on paper. If you don't have time, take a few seconds to mentally assess whether it's smarter to politely say no to avoid overwork, stress, financial overload, or any other discomfort.

2. **Be sensible.** Is it worth risking your physical health to avoid saying no? Overwork and too much stress can jeopardize your overall productivity and your long-term health and happiness. If you want to be more productive, healthier, and less stressed, tell yourself that it's sensible to say no.

3. **Delay.** Give yourself time to consider a request before you say yes or no. If you are approached near the end of a workday, ask, "May I answer this question in the morning?" This will give you time to say no, with compelling reasons to support your refusal. If you can't wait until the next morning, ask whether you can reply in a few minutes. Then breathe deeply, focus on your goals, and prepare your answer.

4. **Add a positive to a negative.** When you say no, add a positive to lessen any ill will or negative reactions to your "no." Examples: "I must say no because I want to do the best job I can on the project I am already working on"; "Tomorrow is a critical day, so I must be rested and energized to put forward my best for you. Respectfully, I must decline"; "I think it's wonderful that you are collecting money for a gift for Mr. X. I don't know Mr. X very well, but I will remember to congratulate Mr. X in person on that day."

5. **Decorate your no with good manners.** When you say no, use polite language to minimize any ill will. Say, "I'm sorry." Say, "I respect you and wish I could say yes." Say, "please" and "thank you" throughout your conversation.

6. **Be ready with a compromise.** When a superior asks you at five minutes before the end of the workday to do extra work, ask whether you can consider this after you have completed a project that's already in the works or when you have rested enough to be energized and ready with your best answer. Ask whether you can share the extra workload with your superior or with another colleague. Ask whether you can take the extra time to do a better job during work hours at a later date. Add a compromise to your no, and you will minimize a poor response to your very sensible no.

Saying No after Work

Difficulty in saying no also applies to home and lifestyle decisions that take place before and after work. Be honest with yourself before saying yes to any request. Ask yourself, "Can I practically respond to this request in a timely manner that will not cause me undue stress?" Taking an extra minute to internally focus on a request will give you the time you need to honestly assess and respond to a request. Take that extra minute.

Match Your Values with Your Goals

If you have high values but no real goals, you will not feel motivated to pursue your work. If you have low values and ambitious goals, you won't derive real satisfaction from your work. You may want to ask yourself, "Which are more important, my goals or my values?" Make the necessary changes to match your values with your goals.

Transform Your Problems into Goals

Problems cause tension and stress, while goals give you motivation. A valuable goal creates positive energy. When you can change your problems to goals, you will accomplish more, be more productive, and feel more enthusiasm for life.

Here are a few ways you can do this:

1. "I have a problem. I don't get along well with my boss."

   Transform the problem into a goal:

   "My goal is to get along better with my boss."

2. "I have a problem. I don't have enough money."

   Transform the problem into a goal:

   "My goal is to earn more money."

3. "I have a problem. I say yes too frequently and get stressed out as a result."

   Transform the problem into a goal:

   "My goal is to say no more often."

---

daily aspiration   "I feel comfortable speaking up when the workload becomes too stressful."

---

33 winding down after work

Workplace stress and anxiety that affect performance on the job can also have a negative impact on the hours that follow the workday. More than three-fourths of the people surveyed by the Anxiety Disorders Association of America reported that stress at work carries over to their personal lives, particularly among women (83 percent of women versus 72 percent of men). Seven in ten of those surveyed reported that workplace stress affects their personal relationships.

The goal is to "turn it off" after work.

dear diva

"I can't turn it off. I spend too many hours stressing on the job, and then I'm supposed to drop it and relax when I go home. It's too hard. How can I leave work and not take stress home with me?"

secrets from the de-stress diva

1. **Visualize a stress-free evening.** Before you leave work, visualize a stress-free evening at home or with friends. Visualize yourself winding down and relaxing, and you'll seek out activities that will allow you to turn your vision into reality.

2. **Create and use a stress-free zone.** Create a stress-free zone in a room or a section of a room, and make it your refuge to relax. Remove computers, and turn off phones and televisions. Create a relaxing mood with simply arranged, comfortable furniture, a good book, a place to set a relaxing cup of caffeine-free tea or a large glass of water, and soft lighting. Let others in your home know that this is your after-work refuge, even if you allow yourself only a few minutes to indulge.

3. **Cut back on television.** Negative news reports are not the only stressful TV fare; another culprit is advertising—commercials that are loud, disruptive, and stress-inducing because they conjure up images suggesting that you have diseases that must be cured or needs that must be met or that taunt you with visions of vacations and possessions you can't afford and don't need. Each day, vow to cut back television time until you are spending some evenings not watching television at all.

4. **Spend five minutes with your journal.** Use your stress-free zone or merely five minutes at a desk or a kitchen table writing down the stresses of your day. Also take the time to celebrate the good things in your life. Then close the journal to free your mind for a peaceful evening ahead.

5. **Enlist your family to de-stress your evenings.** Spend a few minutes sharing chores with your children or spouse, or share meal-preparation duties. You'll begin to look forward to the quality time you can spend with family members, discussing your day and your hopes for the future while you complete chores more quickly.

6. **Simplify your surroundings.** Spend ten minutes each day cleaning and also de-cluttering. Each day, resolve to get rid of a stress-inducing piece of clutter by throwing it away or placing it in a "donations" box that you keep in your car trunk to give later to a shelter or another nonprofit organization. Let go of belongings that are causing you stress, and make room for a less stressful evening.

7. **Don't stress the little messes.** Resolve not to become stressed out at the little messes that might greet you upon your arrival at home. How many people do you know who are perfect? Instead of rolling your eyes and overreacting when you see a mess, smile at the fact that it's human nature to make little messes.

Relax Yourself to Sleep

To enjoy a more healthful night's sleep, relax yourself to the point that you will gently fall asleep.

- Don't engage in vigorous exercise at night. Instead, practice gentle stretching and deep breathing exercises.
- Avoid heavy meals at night; instead, reach for a calming cup of caffeine-free tea.
- Avoid caffeine after noon.
- If a challenging conversation erupts at night, postpone it until the next day to allow yourself time to rest, reflect, and awake more energized in order to respond thoughtfully.
- Turn off the lights and all technological devices at bedtime, make sure that the bedroom is cool, and ease into your bed.

How to De-Stress Evening Meals

Evening meals should be a relaxing time to share a healthy meal. Here are some tips that can help you to de-stress your mealtimes.

Keep it simple. Choose simple meals with healthy ingredients over stressful, time-consuming recipes. You will have more time to spend with your family or relax by yourself.

Discourage negative gossip at the table. Instead, ask family members or friends to share their happiest moment at work or play.

Make television and phone calls off limits during mealtimes.
Share a motivational quote. Ask others to offer a favorite
quote, too.
Ban criticism from the table. Instead, be a role model for
voicing praise.
Be thankful. Use mealtime as an occasion to thank family
members or friends for being an important part of your life.
Thank them for joining you at your table.
Celebrate mealtimes by making your table reflect your joy.
Add a bouquet of flowers or greens from your garden, or
decorate to celebrate the season. Even a bowl of healthful
fruit can make a wonderful centerpiece. Ask family members to take turns being in charge of creating a cheerful
centerpiece for your table.

Living in the Present

Resolve to spend your hours after work living in the present,
instead of focusing on past wrongs or worries. Use your time and
energy constructively. If you find it difficult to do this, think of
two of life's blessings and write them down to inspire yourself to
celebrate the good things that exist in the "now" in your life.

daily aspiration   "I look forward to going home
and relaxing."

money matters

34 taking responsibility for your money

The federal government's U.S. National Income and Product Accounts report states that private savings are at their lowest levels since the Great Depression. At the same time, economists are increasingly sounding the alarm about the fact that few people have the money and the money-management skills to adequately prepare for retirement in an era of disappearing pensions and skyrocketing health costs. Financial hardship is becoming the norm for the vast majority of low- to middle-income populations. Indeed, a major survey by the American Psychological Association found that nearly 75 percent of Americans cite money as a significant source of stress.

dear diva

"I make decent money, but there's never quite enough to pay all the bills at the end of the month. How can I improve my money management?"

secrets from the de-stress diva

Chronic stress subtracts years from your life, shriveling your healthy cells to prematurely speed the deterioration of your body. Why add more wrinkles by worrying about money? Itemize, simplify, and organize your finances to better manage your present and future lifestyles.

Smart money-management skills can alleviate the financial stress in your life.

Katana Abbott, a financial analyst and the cofounder of www. smartwomenscoaching.com and www.designateddaughters.com, said to make the decision to take control of your finances. Here are highlights of what she suggests:

1. Pay yourself first.
   - Make sure you have a cash reserve or an emergency fund. The rule of thumb is enough money to pay at least three months'

worth of fixed expenses, such as rent or mortgage payments, utilities, auto payments, credit cards, food, gasoline, and so forth. Start this savings fund now, even if you can save only $10 a week. Then increase it as you take control.

- Next, you will want to sign up to participate in your employer's retirement plan (like a 401k) *immediately*. If you're self-employed, start to save now. Katana recommends that women save more than men because women outlive men and often take time out of the workforce to care for both children and aging parents.

2. Respect money and control your debt.

- Take a look at your credit cards. Do you pay them off every month? Do you pay your bills on time? Are you in debt and paying only the minimum payment? If you are having problems, get help immediately and stop spending now.

- Buy yourself a small journal, and track your spending for one week so that you can see where the "spending leaks" are: late fees, movie rentals, lattés, fast food, or stuff that you don't really need. These are the dollars that you are going to use to begin to pay off your debt and build up a cash reserve.

- If you start saving $4 a day at age twenty at 10 percent interest, that could potentially accumulate to $1 million. Wait until age thirty and you will need to save $11 a day, and at forty it's $30 a day and at fifty it's $95 a day. So get serious and start now!

3. Assess your job or career path.

- How is your income affecting the rest of your life and your finances?

- Are you passionate about your work, or is it just a job?

- Are you making the best use of your unique talents and skills?

- Are you being paid what you are worth?

- Would you still do your job if you won the lottery or had a magic wand? If the answer is no, then why are you still doing it?

4. Create your game plan.

- Write down your goals for this year.

- Make them clear and specific and give a time frame so that you can track your success.

- Put your list of goals where you can read them, and focus on them every day. You attract what you focus on the most, so focus on what you want in your life daily.
5. Find support and accountability.
  - Surround yourself with positive, supportive people.
  - Find a life coach or a mentor.
  - Hire a financial planner and meet regularly.
  - Read self-improvement books, and get smart about money.
  - Get help on the Internet with a virtual community forum group.
  - Take an educational teleclass that focuses on money, career, or starting a business.

De-Stress

A few drops of essential oil in your bath water provides many therapeutic benefits, from clearing your thoughts to helping with sore and tired muscles.

Relaxing Bath
6 drops geranium
4 drops Roman chamomile
2 drops bois de rose
1 teaspoon Solubol

Add the oils to the Solubol. Fill the tub and pour in the mixture. Soak in the warm bath for fifteen minutes. For a relaxing child's bath, use half the amount of essential oils in the bath water.
Or:
Blend the oils with your favorite carrier oil (one ounce) or unscented lotion, and use this as a body moisturizer.

Listening to Your Intuition

The phone rings and it's the friend whom you were thinking about the other day. Or maybe you leave the house, then get the feeling you should go back home to check the stove because you forgot to turn it off. These are situations where your intuition is at work.

Intuition is a mind-body connection that helps you to make good choices, if you know what to "listen" to. You can start by asking yourself this question every day: "How can I make the necessary small changes to save money?" You will get answers. Dr. Judith Orloff, in her book *Guide to Intuitive Healing: 5 Steps to Physical, Emotional and Sexual Wellness*, said that "gut feelings should be "clear and neutral," and if they are emotional, then you may be coming from fear, rather than from intuition.

daily aspiration
"Money management comes easily to me."

35 paying bills

When bills are due, your stress thermometer may hit the boiling point. One Ohio State University study found that when it comes to paying bills, 40 percent of the people whom researchers surveyed reported that paying bills was "sometimes or always a problem" that contributed to daily stress. Procrastination only worsens stress when overdue bills arrive with late fees attached, making bill payers feel even more overwhelmed.

dear diva

"I fall behind in paying my bills and end up paying late fees extra money we don't have to waste. . . . What is the best way for me to keep up with my bills that will work with my personality and lifestyle?"

secrets from the de-stress diva

There are less stressful ways to approach how you pay your bills.
    The best method of filing or paying bills before they pile up is to keep up with the incoming flow.

Here are a few ideas to downshift the stress of paying bills and eliminate accompanying late fees.

- Create a bill station, where you have all of your bills to be paid in one area.
- Put bills in the bill station every day; take them from the mailbox to the bill station.
- Divide bills into categories such as Home, Insurance, Work, Magazines, Utilities, Phone, and so on. The more specific you are, the easier it will be to file for taxes.
- Set aside one to two hours a week, every week, to pay bills. Rarely will you need more time than this if you keep up with them weekly.
- Take advantage of automatic bill paying via the Internet for monthly bills, such as mortgages, utilities, phone, and so forth. This will save you time during the month.

Pay Yourself First

When you get your paycheck, remember to take out 10 percent off the top. If you're in your own business, this 10 percent may be the only income you receive for yourself after expenses. You can take this 10 percent and invest it or save it.

Time Is Money

Here is an interesting fact about time and money: you can make more money, but you can't make more time. Treat time as if you were paying an employee on an hourly basis. (How true!) This will help you to focus on the quality of time in your life and how you're spending your time.

Remember to relax and enjoy your loved ones. No amount of money is as valuable as the time you spend with your friends and family.

Shave Off Some "Extras"

Let's say you want to travel next year, and you need $300 or $3,000. What will it take to save that money? You could spend $10 a week less ($1.42 a day less), and that would put $520 in your pocket in a year's time without much stress. If you shaved off $20 a week for a year, you would have $1,040 to spend on your vacation. If you put your "shaved savings" in a bank to accumulate interest, you would have even more.

36 getting out of debt

Call it debt stress. Using disposable income to pay off debt is at a historic high. Not only is high debt bad for your bank account, it's bad for your health. A study by Ohio State University found that people who have a high level of stress because of looming debts also suffer more physical impairments than those who pay their bills on time. The greater the debt and the higher the interest rates, the worse a person's health becomes, the researchers said.

One 2002 study by American Express found that 61 percent of working Americans reported feeling moderate to high levels of financial stress, and that credit card debt was a major factor. Unlike in previous decades, your credit report today can affect your ability to get a job because an increasing number of employers check your credit rating in addition to your references. This makes having a poor credit rating especially stressful in an era of downsizing and shrinking numbers of full-time jobs with decent pay.

Your credit rating also affects your ability to rent apartments or homes, just as it has always affected the cost of buying a home. People with poor credit ratings in some states, such as California, are often required to pay the equivalent of the first and the last month's rent, in addition to an exorbitantly high down payment that can triple the cost of renting an apartment. Yet there are ways to organize and proactively manage paying your bills without going into more debt, while at the same time reducing stress. Here's how.

dear diva

"I feel overwhelmed by debts, especially when I face high interest rates. I lose sleep every night over my rising debts. How can I avoid debts and still pay for the things I need, such as health insurance, housing, repairs, child care, transportation, and other expenses?"

secrets from the de-stress diva

An enormous cottage industry has sprung up during the last two decades offering credit counseling, mostly for a fee (which can be negotiated, especially if you have a low income). The public library has dozens of books available that provide step-by-step advice, with worksheets, to help you whittle down your credit card debt. Here are some self-help tips, based in part on research and reports published by Virginia State University and the Virginia Cooperative Extension Service:

1. **Enlist your family.** Enlist the support of your family to honestly assess your debt crisis, and proactively participate in a plan to reduce all unnecessary spending. Start to close charge accounts. Stop using credit cards unless it's for an emergency. Be blunt. For example, ask your child whether it is more important to participate in a certain extracurricular activity or to have a roof over his head.

2. **Be honest with creditors.** Explain that you are overwhelmed with debt. A client who received no help when he asked his creditors for assistance later called them back and said that he was considering bankruptcy. That magic word was all it took for most of his creditors to immediately reduce his interest rates and arrange a longer-term plan of repayment.

3. **Plan your expenses to match your income.** Erase all thoughts of impulse buys, and only make purchases that are absolutely necessary.

4. **Consult a consumer credit counseling service.** They now exist in every state, in every large city, and in most or near smaller communities. Even if you decide not to attend classes, visit the Web sites of these services since many contain free debt-reduction tips.

5. **Create a debt-repayment plan on paper.** List debts in one column and details of your repayment plan in another. Add a third column for disposable income, and a fourth to list necessities such as food.

6. **Revisit your debt-repayment plan often.** Review your plan at least once every thirty or sixty days to make any necessary revisions. Once you start to pare down expenses and stop yourself from using credit cards, you will find that it becomes easier to make additional cuts in your spending.

7. **Practice patience.** Getting out of debt comes with no quick fixes. By actively involving your family in eliminating debt, you are also becoming a valuable role model for your children, which will help them to avoid stress from debt in their adult lives.

8. **Simplify your life.** Stress can rob you of the pleasure that you think will come from spending extra money on vacations or personal items, especially when that spending only exacerbates your debt. Stress also leads to serious health problems, and there is no faster-rising expense than health care. Be smart. Simplify.

Pay Cash

Cut up all of your credit cards, but keep one for emergencies only. For everything else, pay cash. You will be amazed at how much more difficult it is to part with cash than it is to use a credit card for purchases.

Meridian Tapping

Vanessa Wesley, a wellness coach, said, "Meridians are the energy pathways of the body. They're like highway systems in our bodies. Many of my colleagues have said that they feel that tapping on certain meridian pathways is as effective as acupuncture."

"There are seven meridian points on the body that when tapped may alleviate the emotional stress you feel," says Vanessa. These seven meridian points are:

1. Outside of the eyebrow (move from the nose and follow your eyebrow outward)
2. Inside the eyebrow (near the bridge of your nose)
3. Underneath the eye (the soft spot above the cheek bone)
4. Underneath the nose, above the lip (in the center)
5. The bottom of your lip (center)

6. A little lower than the collar bone (move your fingers down your throat to the "v" part and then four inches horizontally to either side)
7. Four inches under the armpit

Try this tapping method:

1. First, think up a statement that names your problem; for example, "I don't have enough money to pay my bills."
2. Identify on a scale from 1 to 10 (with 10 being the most stressful) the degree of stress that you feel.
3. Now, go through the seven meridian pathways, tapping six to seven times with your right or left hand, using your first two fingers (pointer and middle finger), and tap as you repeat the statement that names your problem.
4. When you've completed a round of meridian tapping on all seven points, identify where you are on the stress scale: 1 to 10. For more information on meridian tapping and the Emotional Freedom Technique, go to www.EFT.com.

> daily aspiration   "I have more than enough money to pay my bills on time every month."

37 de-stress retirement plans

Pensions and retirement health plans are going by the wayside in the United States, as more companies eliminate these benefits. A survey by the American Financial Service found two chief stress-inducers for older people: worrying about whether they will have enough money to cover their retirement years, and fearing that they won't be able to pay their medical bills.

The higher cost of living and the decline in the real value of dollars paid for work performed only add to the stress. Many people report that their day-to-day expenses and the increased costs of health care drain their bank accounts of money that should be set aside for retirement. According to the survey, fewer than one in five workers has a professionally prepared financial plan. The challenge is especially acute for working women because the U.S. Department of Labor reported that more women than men work in part-time jobs that do not offer pensions or 401(k) savings plans. Meanwhile, Social Security taxes continue to rise, even as economists predict financial shortfalls for the Social Security system in coming years—a challenge compounded by our aging population that will further strain the system.

The U.S. Department of Labor reports that you will need to replace 70 to 90 percent of your pre-retirement income to maintain your standard of living. That means if you're making $50,000 a year, you will need $35,000 to $45,000 a year in retirement income. I think that is too low since the value of wages in adjusted dollar values has been declining since the 1970s for most jobs, even as we are experiencing enormous increased costs in necessities such as transportation, food, and health care.

Another sign that the Department of Labor's rule of thumb might not work for most older Americans is that even those who have retired with pensions and adequate savings are suddenly returning to work in unprecedented numbers merely to cover the higher costs of prescription medications. Affordable housing is not affordable for almost half of the people in the United States today; how can that same housing be affordable to those same people on retirement, even if they can save enough to cover 70 to 90 percent of their pre-retirement income?

Is there a way to begin planning now to stave off disaster in your "golden years"?

dear diva

"It seems that every cent I earn goes toward my everyday living expenses, such as health care, food, transportation, and housing. When an emergency strikes, what little I have saved disappears. It all seems so hopeless. How can I save for retirement?"

secrets from the de-stress diva

1. **Acknowledge the challenge.** Read, research, and understand the many difficulties involved in putting aside enough money to retire. Don't allow the dismal statistics to paralyze you; make the decision to consider this a challenge that you can positively address to reach your goals.

2. **Downsize your retirement goals.** Pensions were the mainstay of your parents' generation; most Americans who don't work at government jobs will have no pensions or they might possess 401(k) plans, which may be overly dependent on a volatile stock market. Think smaller in terms of housing, recreation, travel, and other traditional retirement goals.

3. **Double your savings, right now.** Put yourself on a budget you can live with, whether you are in your twenties or your fifties. Take proactive steps to minimize stress. It is never too late to increase your savings. Simplify your life and put off major purchases. Once you double your savings, consider further adjustments to increase your savings, one step at a time.

4. **Make retirement your priority.** You will age, and the Social Security system cannot cover the high cost of living. Period.

5. **Consult a financial planner.** Even if you cannot afford to make large investments in a retirement portfolio, comparison shop for the services of a financial consultant who can offer an expert outside opinion on how you can proceed, whether you have a huge stock portfolio or only $50 in your bank account. A session with a financial consultant is money well spent because retirement is an essential priority in your life.

6. **Diversify your retirement investments.** Case in point: the people whose 401(k) or personal investments were made in Enron. They lost everything. Diversifying your investments in savings bonds, savings accounts, stocks, real estate, or other sources also minimizes your risk.

Go Back to School

Many community colleges offer continuing education classes on finances that also focus on retirement planning. A good number of these classes are free or low in cost. Knowledge is a powerful weapon against the stress of inaction and ignorance. Empower yourself with knowledge.

Update Your Skills

The vast majority of Americans do not have the resources to retire at fifty-five or sixty-five or even at older ages, as did past generations. Update your skills to be ready to reenter the workforce if necessary. The bonus is that an active mind is a powerful antiaging deterrent, in addition to being a practical investment in your future.

Simplify Your Life

Eliminating extravagances now will prepare you to live a happier retirement. Start checking out resources that you overlooked in the past; for example, borrow DVDs from the library, rather than renting or buying them; take advantage of coupons online or in the paper; go grocery shopping every ten days instead of every week to eliminate unnecessary purchases; make cappuccinos and lattés at home.

> daily aspiration   "I'm saving money every month to put in my retirement savings."

38 finding a new home

Buying or renting a new home can be as stressful as starting or losing a job. Housing costs take up a major part of most budgets. In a fluctuating housing market, your stress meter can go haywire. That's because the traditional reason for buying a home, as an investment that will only increase in value, has suddenly become a high-risk venture in regions where housing values are plummeting. High risk equals danger equals high stress.

Renting, too, is stressful. Rents continue to rise through the ups and downs of housing markets, and squeezed real estate owners will often raise rents as high as possible to make up for higher payments that are due on adjustable-rate mortgages.

How much space do you need? How much space can you afford? How high will interest rates go? How do you factor in changing jobs—and people change jobs more often during their careers than did previous generations—and being forced to move to a new location?

dear diva

"Rents have risen dramatically, and so many people I know who purchased houses are now watching their home values plummet. I feel overwhelmed by the thought of making a wrong decision that will ruin my finances. How can I afford to pay for my home?"

secrets from the de-stress diva

There are ways for you to de-stress this major decision and make a smart choice.

1. **Do your homework.** Make a decision whether to rent or buy. Where you live is most often determined by where you work. With people changing jobs more often than in any other generation, take into consideration whether you should rent or buy, based on that fact. Can you buy a house and afford to sell it should you have to change jobs and move to another location, especially in a region with plummeting sale prices? Should you rent for the first few months to give yourself ample time to shop for a house in the right neighborhood?

2. **Consult a local real estate professional and then another.** It's free, and you will receive expert advice on local rental and home sale prices, whether you decide to use that agent or another. Empower yourself with knowledge, and you'll instantly downshift your stress regarding this major decision.

3. **Investigate the neighborhood first.** Police stations keep crime statistics that are based on zip codes. Visit the local police station to gather important information that will help you make your

decision. Cities and states rate public and private schools by test scores, safety, and other factors. Invite yourself to a neighborhood PTA meeting or social gathering and ask the people in attendance about the neighborhood. If you rent or buy a house in a neighborhood that is unsafe, has poor schools, or is unkempt, your bargain will ultimately prove to be no bargain at all.

4. **If you are renting, investigate your landlord.** Is your potential landlord someone who will want to enter your house at will or who is not around when repairs are needed? With luck, you can find a former tenant who will truthfully answer your concerns. Stress-free renters tend to have likable, accessible, and responsible landlords.

5. **Play house detective.** Write down everything that is wrong or in disrepair and ask whether repairs can be made before you move in. If not, can you negotiate a lower price if you are able to improve the value of the house or the apartment yourself?

6. **Consider the transportation factor.** When gas prices were cheap, suburbs were more attractive, even if they were thirty or forty miles away from your job. Factor in the cost of your commute when deciding whether to rent or buy a home.

7. **Don't be an impulse buyer (or renter).** Just as you can rue an impulse buy at a department store or a hardware complex, you can rue an impulse decision to rent or buy a home based on a first impression. Don't allow yourself to be pressured by a seller or an agent who insists that "this one will go fast." A hasty decision can lay the groundwork for a great deal of stress over the course of a lease or a long-term mortgage. The risk of losing a "fast deal" is far less than the long-term cost of making a bad decision.

Let Go

Try to let go of your worries about finding a home to rent or buy. Once you have taken the previous steps, you need to let go of the worries, the regrets, or the fears you may have about getting your new home. How? By letting the process work and not trying to control every little detail of what might go wrong with the home. Notice the negative comments, the old hurts, and other concerns pulling you down during this time. Finding the right home may trigger these old thinking patterns.

Consider the Energy-Efficiency Factor

The cost of energy can add an enormous expense to the mortgage payment or the rent if your potential home does not have energy-efficient features. Even a dilapidated refrigerator can add hundreds of dollars to your electric bill each year.

> daily aspiration
> "I love where
> I am living."

39 selling a home with less stress

Selling a home is a stressful event, especially when a real estate boom goes bust. Selling can also be time-consuming and especially stressful for already time-starved workers and families. If a house does not immediately sell, the stress becomes magnified. Home sellers also report feeling anxious about a lack of privacy that occurs when Open Houses allow strangers to suddenly have access to your house. What steps can you take to make selling a home less stressful?

dear diva

"I feel exhausted by all the work that will go into selling my home, and I feel uncomfortable allowing strangers inside my house. Property values are going down in so many states; I feel that this will impact me adversely, which only adds to my stress. How can I sell my house for the best price, in the shortest amount of time, and with the least degree of stress?"

secrets from the de-stress diva

Planning ahead can alleviate much of the stress in selling a house, even in a "down" market. Veteran realtors advise that most buyers take their first impressions very seriously, so if your house makes a good first impression, this can cut down on the time it takes for a buyer to decide and to close the deal.

1. **Hire a Realtor carefully.** Treat retaining a Realtor as you would hiring any other important employee. Prepare a list of questions, and take your time interviewing a Realtor (or a real estate professional). Discuss your goals with the person you are considering, and ask how this applicant can meet them. Check references. Engage the services of a Realtor who is experienced at selling homes in your community. Comparison shop. Interview three top candidates and choose the best of the three based not only on skill, but on a reasonable commission.

2. **Get your house ready at least thirty days before you post the "For Sale" sign.** Many Realtors agree that it takes thirty days to get a house ready because first impressions will often prove to be the most important factor in whether a "looker" eventually becomes a "buyer." Make the investment in external repairs that can mean the difference between a buyer leaving with a quick no and spending extra time examining your house. You need to professionally paint, patch, and repair the areas that buyers will see first.

3. **Consult the owners of homes that successfully sold.** The features that buyers consider valuable can vary from region to region. Ask people in your community who have newly placed "sold" signs in their yards for pointers on how to prepare your house for sale. What did they notice that most "lookers" paid attention to or commented on, when exploring their house? Ask for advice on whether a new carpet seemed more important than a fresh coat of paint on the walls. Take lots of notes. These can serve as your guide to using your time wisely to prepare your home for sale.

4. **Actively engage your family.** Let them know that there will be "company" and that they need to assist you with their unique skills. Let the list maker in your family make lists of repairs and "sprucing up" chores and also keep lists of Open House dates and other important information. Let the decorator in your family help you to arrange furniture, decide on window dressings, and place inviting accessories throughout your home to show off its advantages. Let the handyman (or the handywoman) be in charge of sprucing up the yard and the garage and making repairs. Delegating the work that goes into selling a home will dramatically reduce your stress.

5. **Disappear your pets (temporarily, of course).** Not everyone likes dogs; not everyone likes cats. On Open House days, arrange for your pets to spend a day away in a boarding facility or visiting a member of your family.

6. **Be honest.** No house is perfect. Be honest about shortcomings. The buyer will trust your honesty and will be more inclined to decide to make a purchase.

7. **Be patient.** The higher the price, the longer it will take to sell your home. Have a frank discussion with your agent about what amount you will accept below the asking price or how long it will take to find a buyer who will meet your price.

De-Clutter

A cluttered house looks smaller. Rent a temporary space at a local storage facility and fill it with seasonal items you don't need immediate access to, out-of-season clothes, and even extra furniture. It's a small investment to make if you can then offer a spacious home for sale, rather than a cramped one. A de-cluttered house will also reduce your stress levels by simplifying the sprucing-up process. Place personal items out of sight.

De-Stress Your House

Exchange harsh lighting for soft lighting. Veteran real estate professionals swear by the smell of freshly baked cookies. Use an inviting, but not overpowering, scent in each room. Sprinkle baking soda on your carpet before you vacuum to absorb any odors. Buy a bouquet of fresh flowers such as daisies to brighten up your dining room. As a bonus, de-stressing your house will also de-stress you. A relaxed, stress-free homeowner can be just as strong a selling point as a spotless kitchen.

Be Flexible

From the time that the "For Sale" sign goes up, plan in advance to be flexible about activities that won't distract from your main goal. Don't schedule messy parties or major functions during this period because you want your home to be tidy at all times.

Tell your family that you will start to prepare your home for sale thirty days before the "For Sale" sign goes up, which means that you must plan important activities sixty days in advance.

Keep a Dream Journal

Ask yourself a question before you go to sleep. When you wake up, record anything you remember about your dreams. You may want to ask yourself before going to sleep, "How can I lessen the stress in my life?" Chances are good that you will start to have insights about how to solve your problem.

daily aspiration   "We sold our home very quickly."

relax and energize your body

40 start your day with a smile on the inside

We all have so much on our plates in modern life, with days that overflow with responsibilities and activities. Even though some technological advances have cut down on the time we spend doing certain daily chores, other devices may create more stress than relief in our lives. For example, through the Internet and other means of communication, we are able to remain in touch with others on a global scale, yet having to do business with people who live in different time zones can mess with our circadian or natural rhythms.

Studies have shown that stress suppresses the immune system and has been linked to a variety of diseases and disorders, such as type 2 diabetes, chronic fatigue syndrome, and cancer. Yet sometimes a quick and simple change of perception can transform your mental state from stressed to calm. Try this the next time you find yourself stressed during the day:

Sit quietly.

Notice your breathing—is it fast or slow?

Take a calm, deliberate breath in and then slowly exhale. Continue to do this as you go through the following mental exercise.

Think of today as a bright new day. It doesn't matter what the weather is outside because you're inside, where you're protected from heat, wind, humidity, snow, or the wind. Most of us do not have to walk miles in the snow to get to school or work, as our grandparents and parents might have done. Even though the weather may not be exactly the way you prefer, the passing seasons keep you aware of the flow of time. And since each season has its own richness, if you focus on this, rather than on the weather on a specific day, you will be able to enjoy any type of weather that occurs outside of your safe refuge, your home.

Say to yourself, "I'm going to reframe what just made me feel stressed."

Example: Maybe you feel stressed because you don't have a high level of self-confidence right now, and it has prevented you from moving forward on something you want to do.

Instead of saying to yourself, "I can't [do such and such]," I want you to think of a time when you assumed that you couldn't do something but then you did it. Many times, this will help you to reframe the situation and get a "reality check." This technique might make you realize that you can change "I can't" to "I can and I did." Sometimes, it takes very little impetus to move yourself through your self-imposed emotional blockages.

dear diva

"There is so much I need to do today, I don't know where to start first. I feel completely stressed out. How can I face my day without being paralyzed by stress?"

secrets from the de-stress diva

- Find a small ball, about six inches in diameter, and roll it between your hands when you feel stressed. This is a great way to calm your jitters without drinking another cup of coffee or eating "comfort foods" in order to relax.

- Keep one or two uplifting and inspirational songs on your iPod, and when you feel stressed during the day, take a few minutes to listen to one or both of the songs . . . and if you can, go to your car or a soundproof conference room and sing along loudly!

- Plan your day. You may have the best intentions of getting things done today, contacting people you need to reach, and picking up items that need to be picked up. But if you don't put together a daily plan, then three things usually happen: (1) you waste time trying to get centered and focused on what needs to be done for the day; (2) you'll check your e-mail because that is simply a habit and wastes time; and/or (3) you'll lose your motivation to work on your tasks because you feel as if there just isn't enough time to get them all done. This becomes a self-fulfilling prophecy.

- Identify the two top-priority items on your to-do list. In other words, if you had no time to do anything else, by doing these two things you would feel as if you accomplished something at the end of the day. When you complete two items in each category (tasks, calls, e-mails), go on to the next two items. I call this the Rule of Two.

- Do something for yourself every day, even if that means sipping a cappuccino while reading your favorite paper or magazine for ten minutes or belting out one of your favorite songs while driving to work in the morning. It doesn't require a lot of time; you merely need to remember to do something you enjoy every day.

- One of the fastest and best ways to instantly change any negative attitude or thought is to use *gratitude*: focus on one thing you are grateful for. It will immediately put you on a more positive track.

- Once a week, put a new outfit together. Maybe you can combine a blouse with a skirt or a pair of pants that you've never worn together before. This is an excellent time to make use of accessories such as belts and fun jewelry. This mix and match accomplishes three things: (1) it gives you a new look; (2) it helps you to think outside the box and, in so doing, to expand your wardrobe; and (3) it helps you to get out of a routine or a rut.

- There is something beautiful and empowering in starting your day with a heartfelt ritual.

  1. Say a grateful sentence upon awakening, while you're still in bed
  2. Get up, stretch your hands overhead, and breathe in slowly and deeply. Repeat this three times.
  3. Meditate for five to ten minutes
  4. Create your mantra for the day. One that resonates with me is "The gift is in the present." What is yours?

Aromatherapy

When you find that you are overwhelmed and need a little space to breathe, place a few drops of eucalyptus essential oil on a paper towel and breathe in.

Food

B vitamins help to turn food into energy and are sometimes considered the de-stress vitamins. Some foods that are rich in B vitamins are brown rice, oatmeal, apricots, broccoli, blueberries, asparagus, bananas, garbanzo beans, grapes, kale, onions, and passion fruit.

Relaxation

We know that stress suppresses our immune systems. New research has shown that men and women who take a half-hour nap at least three times a week had a 37 percent reduced risk of dying from heart disease (*Archives of Internal Medicine*, study author Androniki Naska, PhD).

> daily aspiration
> "I am so fortunate to have such a full life."

41 great ways to start your day

Mornings set the mood for your entire day.
   What happens in the first few hours of your day sets the stage for the rest of the day. This is why it is essential that you do not watch the news or read the daily paper first thing in the morning, unless it has to do with business, cultural events, and so forth.

Those of us who skip eating a healthy breakfast also set ourselves up for a high-stress day. Researchers have found many potential ill effects caused by skipping the first meal of the day, such as impaired memory, negative attitudes, and a decline in mental endurance. One New Zealand study reports that people who skip breakfast are more likely to catch a cold or even the flu.

The media thrives on bad news and on creating a problem when one doesn't exist. Sensationalism sells papers and attracts viewers. I'm not suggesting that you shouldn't keep up with the local or international news; just don't do it first thing in the morning as you start your day.

If you feel rushed in the morning or you have to hurry to get others ready, your level of stress has begun to escalate, and it won't take much to get you upset and anxious. There's a lot you can do to keep your stress and anxiety levels down. You will make better decisions and enjoy your life more when you learn to control morning stress.

If you can, train your body to wake up without an alarm. There are a few ways to do this:

1. Go to bed and wake up at about the same time every day, including on weekends.
2. Before you go to sleep, tell yourself the time you want to wake up. You may want to have an alarm clock as a backup until you become confident that you will wake up at the time you requested. Your subconscious is a very powerful partner.

A note about alarms: please use soothing music as your wake-up alarm. No one wants to be startled, let alone first thing in the morning.

dear diva

"I often rush in the mornings and bring that panicked feeling to the office. How can I calm down in the morning?"

secrets from the de-stress diva

Mornings are new beginnings, and you need to take advantage of this. Most of us love new beginnings. The first thing to do upon arising is to think about the fact that you are up and alive.

- **Keep a journal.** Take five minutes and write in a journal or on a legal pad. You can choose to throw out the writing afterward, but it is important that you take a few minutes in the morning to get any negative thoughts out, including confusion or anxiety about what you need to do today. Then, end with two things you're grateful for.
- **Start with affirmations.** Also, use your shower time to say positive affirmations: "This is a great day," "I'm looking forward to having a productive day today," "I'm so grateful for today."

- **Make your day special.** Wear that new skirt or pair of pants or shoes today. If you want to keep something for a special occasion, then wear it today because today is a special occasion!
- **Commit to being happy today.** Say "I do" to life today and make a commitment to yourself to be happy. Regard your agenda and whatever else happens to you today as your "daily cup of life" — and see it as half full, rather than half empty.
- **Make your first phone call positive and affirming.** Call yourself at the office, and leave a message for yourself consisting of a positive, uplifting affirmation. Listen to your voice-mail messages when you get to the office. It will help you stay grounded and "real" for the day.
- **Buy or cut fresh flowers.** Set the mood in your home or at the office with fresh flowers from your garden or from the store. So many convenience stores sell beautiful and reasonably priced flowers.
- **Be kind to yourself.** Imagine you are someone else. Would you berate that person or think poorly of him or her for not finishing the necessary tasks and duties every day? You wouldn't do this, so why do you berate yourself? Try to feel compassion for yourself. Whenever you feel "less than," remember your strengths and talents. If on some mornings you can't think of any good qualities, ask a friend to remind you of them.

Chamomile Tea

Enjoy a cup of chamomile tea to maintain calmness.

Breathe

Stand up or sit. Inhale and exhale with a long, slow breath. Do this two more times, but now raise your hands above your head as you breathe in and then slowly let your arms come down to your sides as you breathe out. You are taking in extra oxygen and letting it circulate throughout your body while you do this breathing exercise.

Food

Make sure you start your morning with breakfast, even though it may take only five minutes to make. You can boil eggs the night before and have two eggs, a half cup of orange juice, and some whole-wheat toast with a little peanut butter. This breakfast has protein that will sustain you and stabilize your blood sugar. A meal consisting mainly of refined carbohydrates digests too quickly and causes a quick spike and then a dip in your blood sugar, at which point you feel starving again.

When you're hungry, it is much harder to concentrate and do good work. Your body tells you when it's hungry for a reason, just as your gas gauge tells you when your car's tank is nearing empty.

Fast, easy breakfasts include fresh fruit, yogurt, and granola; a piece of whole-wheat toast with low-fat cheese and tomato slices on top; and a piece of whole-wheat toast with peanut butter and banana slices on top. For more ideas on easy healthy meals, check out the book *The De-Stress Diva in the Kitchen: Quick, Easy and Healthy Recipes* (www.destressdiva.com).

Or, you can start off your morning with a fruit smoothie. It's much more filling than juice because the fruit has fiber and will sustain you for a longer time. Add some type of protein as well, for an all-around healthy breakfast.

SMOOTHIE RECIPE

Serves 2

1 cup orange juice	½ banana
3 tablespoons nonfat dry milk powder	10 fresh strawberries
	3 tablespoons nonfat yogurt

Combine all of the ingredients in your blender.

Relaxation

Close your eyes and imagine that you are looking out at an ocean or a horizon or into a vast pine-tree forest. Your brain will slow down and will release the stress that comes from focusing too intently on reading, a computer screen, and so on.

> daily aspiration   "I'm enjoying my morning, with nature and activity around me."

42 creating bedtime rituals

You bring the worries of the day to bed with you, and this is what keeps you from having a restful night. Cortisol is a stress hormone linked to depression, high blood pressure, obesity, and other serious health ailments. A recent study by researchers at Northwestern University, published by *Proceedings of the National Academy of Science*, shows that when people experience days that end badly, they can wake up with high levels of cortisol in their bodies.

The study, based on data collected by researchers at the University of Chicago, also reported that people who experience anger throughout the day have higher levels of cortisol at night.

A good night's sleep is one of the best antiaging weapons in your de-stress toolbox. Yet according to one survey by the National Sleep Foundation, more than half (54 percent) of all adults report experiencing at least one symptom of insomnia.

The smart way to get a good night's sleep is with a bedtime ritual. The beauty of rituals occurs when they are firmly established in your life; then you start to look forward to them and actually feel as if something just isn't right when you don't do them. Take advantage of their soulful and joyful usefulness.

dear diva

"I wake up almost every night after about three to four hours of sleep, and then it takes me hours to get back to sleep. Sometimes I can't fall asleep because I'm so worried about what will happen tomorrow. How can I get more rest during the night?"

secrets from the de-stress diva

Bedtime is the perfect time to create downshifting rituals. Your behaviors and responses are very strong when they are attached to certain calming thoughts, smells, and locations. You can literally teach yourself to downshift and get calm before bedtime merely by lighting lavender candles, sipping chamomile tea, or taking deep breaths while you think calm and peaceful thoughts. (Be sure to blow out the candles before you fall asleep.) Creating bedtime rituals that you do every night will encourage this type of conditioning.

1. **Exercise early in the day.** Exercise energizes you for the day ahead and also helps you fall asleep at night because your body needs to rest from the day's exertions. Exercising late in the day negates that goal by energizing you at a time of day when you want to be relaxing . . . unless you exercise at least three hours before going to bed.

2. **Become conscious of your evening eating habits.** Avoid caffeinated products (including chocolate and decaf coffee, because most decaf coffees still have traces of caffeine in them).

3. **Close the book (literally!) on your stress.** Before you go to bed, write about your day, your worries, and your fears about the day ahead in your personal journal or on a piece of paper. Before it's time to go to sleep, close your journal or throw away the piece of paper on which you have written down your problems. You have just closed the book on stressful thoughts that otherwise would keep you up at night.

4. **Visualize yourself relaxed and ready for sleep.** Sit quietly and comfortably in a chair or in a bath and visualize yourself as sleepy. It's not self-hypnosis, merely a way to tell yourself that it's time to consciously relax your muscles and your mind. Tell yourself, out loud, "I am ready to go to sleep."

5. **Strive for dark, quiet, and cool.** Create a quiet, cool environment and turn off all the lights to encourage sleep. Close the curtains. Turn off cell phones, computers, and other electronics. If you live in a hot climate, cool the air with a fan or an air conditioner. This will encourage you to nestle (snuggle up), just as you did as a child.

6. **Establish a sleep clock.** Condition yourself to fall asleep at the same time each night. Eventually, your body will subconsciously and consciously become conditioned to unwind and sleep at a regularly scheduled time.

7. **Sleep like a baby.** Melatonin is a naturally occurring hormone produced by the pineal gland. The level of melatonin in your body lessens as you age, making it more difficult for you to "sleep like a

baby." Today, melatonin has become readily available as a low-cost, natural supplement that's sold in most drugstores and grocery stores. It's a favorite of world travelers, who report that using melatonin helps them to adjust more quickly to changes in time zones that otherwise would disrupt their sleeping schedules. Ask your physician or health-care provider whether melatonin is right for you.

Aromatherapy

Take a warm bath with Epsom salts. If you wish, you can add some aromatherapy essential oils. Add four drops of lavender and four drops of ylang-ylang. Surround your bath with small unscented candles or else those scented with lavender or ylang-ylang. Or add a few drops of vanilla-scented oil to your bath water. (If you are not a fan of candles, there are a number of battery-powered candles on the market. I suggest the Smart Candle, available at www.momastore.org.)

Visualize

Sit quietly and comfortably in a chair or in a bath and think of a large, shiny, warm rock placed on every part of your body that feels tense. Take an inventory of your body's tense areas, starting with your feet, legs, thighs, hips, lower back, middle back, upper back, shoulders, arms, hands, neck, temples, and head. Feel the warm rock opening up and dissolving any tension. Take a deep breath as the rock dissolves each area of tension.

Herbs

Drinking a warm cup of chamomile tea is an excellent way to de-stress before bedtime. The warm tea promotes perspiration, and the herbal compounds of chamomile relax you. While drinking your cup of tea, stay away from the computer and the news on TV. Focus on downshifting for the day. As you sip your chamomile tea, this is a perfect time to think of three things for which you're grateful.

Homeopathy

Dr. Mindy Boxer, a natural health-care provider in Santa Monica, California, says, Coffea Cruda alleviates stress accompanied by obsessive worrying and overthinking.

Potency: 12X or 6C; three pellets dissolved under the tongue. Dr. Boxer also suggests that when symptoms improve, take the remedy less often. Remember, less is more.

> daily aspiration "I look forward to a restful night's sleep."

43 beginning a new exercise regimen

Exercise is a powerful weapon against stress, causing your body to release endorphins, which promote a more powerful sense of well-being and energy. Exercise carries oxygen to your brain. Even as few as ten to twenty minutes of exercise each day can produce measurable benefits. One study in 2000 showed that 20 minutes of aerobic exercise reduces anxiety and can improve moods for up to 40 minutes immediately afterward. Another study by the Center for Research in Disease Prevention in 2001 found that walking for 20 minutes daily for just seven weeks resulted in improvements in mood and increased energy levels that lasted for up to five months. One Stanford University study found that exercising earlier in the day can help adults to fall asleep faster and sleep longer. Another study by Ohio State University proved that regular exercise can help wounds to heal faster by as much as 25 percent.

dear diva

"It's so hard finding the time in my busy day to exercise. How can I make time to exercise every day? It's too much to add this to my already overwhelming lists of tasks. How can I establish an exercise regimen that will reduce stress and make me healthier?"

secrets from the de-stress diva

Sometimes it's just a matter of getting started and then resolving to maximize the benefits of exercise by doing it regularly, starting at twenty minutes every three days and working up to twenty to thirty minutes each day. Of course, if you have a medical condition, consult a physician before you begin any exercise regimen.

1. **Resolve to begin exercising.** Simply resolving to exercise and visualizing yourself exercising every day will create a positive mind-set that will help you to get started and stick to an exercise regimen.

2. **Build your exercise routine slowly.** Just do it. It can be productive even if you exercise five minutes a day by running in place, doing jumping jacks, or taking a short walk to the end of your street and back. Slowly add minutes each day to your exercise routine, as you add more days each week that you spend time exercising. Be patient until you gain the momentum and the strength to extend your exercise periods.

3. **Schedule your exercise.** Create a chart, and pencil in your exercise goals and results. Resolve to exercise twenty minutes each day, either all at once at the beginning of the day or in ten-minute increments at different times of the day. Make a checkmark on your chart after completing your exercise.

4. **Vary your exercise regimen.** On successive days, you can schedule brisk walking, weight-lifting exercises, an active sport such as tennis with a friend, learning a new sport, and taking a yoga or organized exercise class. Vary your routine to keep yourself interested in maintaining the exercise schedule.

5. **Enlist an exercise buddy.** Your exercise buddy can be a friend who joins you for a brisk walk, a game of basketball or tennis, or an exercise class. Or, if you're alone, accompany yourself with upbeat music, inspirational tapes, or books on tape played on a portable CD or cassette player. Yet another tactic is to mentally bring along a

challenge from work or home while you exercise; you can internally address and solve this problem as you exercise.

6. **Don't overdo it.** Sore muscles and a feeling of frustration will sabotage the crucial goal of striving to exercise regularly. When you feel sore, ease up on exercising and focus instead on deep breathing and gentle stretching until the soreness lessens. If you are a beginner, don't feel frustrated if you can't reach your goals yet. Instead, make your daily goals easier until you build up the energy or master the skills to improve your exercise times and intensity.

7. **Skip exercise when you are ill or injured.** Instead, turn to gentle stretching if possible for several minutes a day. Otherwise, just rest, knowing that you can resume your exercise regimen when you feel fit.

8. **Take mini exercise breaks during your work day.** When you answer the phone, stand up and pace or stretch as you talk. Take one-minute stretching breaks. Park your car farther away from your destination to add more walking time. Take the stairs instead of the elevator. When you review paperwork, take it with you on a short walk through the hallways or outside. When you are at your desk, focus on contracting your stomach muscles while you sit up straight for several minutes at a time, to build your core body strength.

Stretching the Right Way

Stretching the right way can be a form of exercise, in and of itself, and can also make muscles and joints limber to help you warm up for exercise and prevent injuries. Stretching increases your flexibility, makes your joints function better, improves your circulation, quickly alleviates stressed thoughts and muscles, and promotes better posture. The goal is to hold each stretch for at least thirty seconds. Look at your watch or at a clock to time your stretching. Don't stretch an injured muscle. Breathe deeply, in and out, as you stretch. Don't stretch to the point of pain.

Integrate Exercise

Integrate exercise into your daily routines.

- While watching television, use weights for strength-building exercises, run in place during commercials, or practice yoga or simple stretching exercises.

- When you answer the phone at home, stand up and walk and stretch as you talk.
- While doing the laundry, take vigorous walks up and down the stairs, through hallways, or around the block between wash and dry cycles.
- Take up gardening, a great stress-buster that is also exercise.
- Walk to the store instead of driving, whenever possible.
- When you talk to your children, walk while you talk. Tell your children that you will be more relaxed and energized to help them if they walk along with you while you both talk.
- When you start your exercise regimen, use these mini exercise sessions to add to the time you spend exercising each day. As you gradually increase the amount of time you exercise, you'll begin to consider these brief exercise breaks to be perks, instead of part of your timed exercise periods.

> daily aspiration   "I enjoy exercising every day."

44 avoiding exercise burnout

Exercise is a powerful weapon against stress. It encourages the production of energizing endorphins, strengthens your immune system, and eases anxiety. Exercise also counters the effects of long-term stress that can raise blood pressure levels and can lead to obesity, which is exacerbated by the stress-related hormone cortisol. But what can you do when exercise burnout happens?

dear diva

"I began exercising to feel better, but now I'm burned out by injuries and the sheer exhaustion of so much exercise. Plus, it has become so tedious. How can I overcome exercise burnout without jeopardizing my health?"

secrets from the de-stress diva

1. **Vary your routine.** Switch from intensive aerobic exercises to weight lifting on one day and yoga on another. This will prevent exercise burnout and boredom, while also ensuring that different muscle groups are exercised regularly to enhance the overall benefits of exercise.

2. **Vary exercise times.** The rote nature of exercising during the same time of day can also contribute to exercise burnout. Exercise at different times of the day. Or, break down forty minutes of exercise each day into twenty- or ten-minute increments.

3. **Get enough sleep.** A lack of adequate sleep can play a strong role in exercise burnout because exhaustion creates stress, fatigue, and a lack of focus that can lead to injuries. Take steps to wind down at night, create a comfortable sleep environment, and try other measures to encourage a good night's sleep. Never do strenuous exercise two or three hours before sleep because this can increase your energy levels and prevent you from being relaxed enough to fall asleep.

4. **Take an exercise class.** You don't have to join a gym in order to take a class. Local community centers, churches, and social groups offer a variety of free or low-cost exercise classes to vary how you exercise, and they also offer a change of scenery.

5. **Get an exercise buddy.** If you don't have an exercise buddy, get one to allow you to socialize while you exercise. Plus, you can strategize together on how to vary your routines to avoid exercise burnout.

6. **Incorporate stretching into your exercise routine.** Stopping to stretch for ten or fifteen minutes can alleviate the boredom and the stress that accompany nonstop intensive exercise. For example, stretch, run for fifteen minutes, spend fifteen minutes doing gentle stretching exercises, and then run for fifteen more minutes. Stretching before and while walking or weight lifting can alleviate burnout.

7. **Take a three-day exercise break.** Rather than give up exercise altogether because of exercise burnout, take a three-day break. This break will not reverse the effects of a long-term exercise routine, but can provide a welcome vacation from exercise that will relax and refresh you and then refocus your attention on exercise.

Burnout-Proof Isometrics

Isometric exercise doesn't lead to the burnout that may result from intensive exercise, which causes you to sweat excessively and possibly suffer injuries. Switching to isometric exercise as an alternative to intense exercise on alternate days or as your sole source of exercise for several days or several months can alleviate exercise burnout. Here are three isometric moves that do not require expensive equipment or long periods of time.

- While seated at your desk, push against the arm rests as if you were lifting yourself out of your chair to exercise your shoulder and arm muscles, while you also relieve tense muscles.

- To do abdominal isometrics, stand up tall, breathe in deeply, and pull in your stomach muscles. It is important not to hold your breath during isometric exercises, but to breathe in and exhale regularly. Breathing in and out while you contract your stomach muscles strengthens different sections of your abdomen. Practice this for several minutes each day at your desk, while standing, or while walking.

- Push your weight against a wall, as if you were doing push-ups, using the wall to contract and strengthen your arm, shoulder, and abdominal muscles. Perform this exercise slowly to maximize your results.

> daily aspiration
> "I look forward to a new exercise program."

45 don't forget your feet

Just as there are seven chakras in the body," said Dr. Vasant Lad, "there are seven chakras in the soles of the feet." And those feet serve us constantly, for we are remarkable walkers. Most Americans walk 5,000 to 7,000 steps a day, but in order to be more healthy you can set a goal of 10,000 steps or more each day. The average person walks about 115,000 miles in a lifetime, more than four times the circumference of the globe. A 150-pound person walking one mile exerts the equivalent of 63.5 tons, or 127,000 pounds, on each foot. That's why, according to the American Podiatric Medical Association, your feet are more subject to injury than any other part of the body.

dear diva

"My feet are sore from walking and standing. How can I make my feet feel better at the end of the day?"

secrets from the de-stress diva

A gentle foot massage is best at bedtime because of its relaxing properties. Use warm, rather than cold, oil because it is more comforting and penetrates the skin more easily. Sit in a chair and have a pair of socks ready to put on after you finish your foot massage.

First, gently massage your right foot. Then gently rub the oil in small, circular motions from your ankle to the toes and the soles of your feet. Next, press your thumb on the spot where your shin meets the top of your foot. Gently and slowly drag your thumb across the top of your foot to the big toe, and then do the same with the other toes. This improves circulation. Now cross your right ankle over your left knee and cup the side of your right heel in your left hand. Place your right hand on the top of the foot, lace your fingers between your toes, and push the foot inward, outward, and then in a circular motion. With your right thumb, apply pressure to your big toe along the inner border of your foot. Then drag your thumb from the root of your fifth toe to the heel. Make a fist with your right hand and press it against the foot, working it along the sole in a circular motion to activate a variety of energy points. Repeat all of these movements on your left foot. Finish your foot massage by soaking your feet for five to ten minutes in a bucket filled halfway with warm water and a teaspoon of Epsom salt, to draw the stress and the toxins out of your feet.

This is a perfect way to downshift after a busy and stressful day. While your feet are soaking, you can write in your journal or read calming and inspirational material.

Aromatherapy

Peppermint oil helps to restore circulation in your feet. Put five drops of peppermint into a foot bath, and soak your feet for about ten to twenty minutes.

Bodywork Exercises

Walk every day and swim as much as possible; these are the best leg exercises. Walk in the ocean, if you can, to absorb strengthening sea minerals. Walk in the early morning dewy grass. Walk on tiptoe around the house. Massage your feet and legs every morning and night with diluted myrrh oil. Elevate your legs whenever possible, even while sitting. Sit with a stool to prop your feet on.

daily aspiration   "My beautiful feet take me where I need to go."

46 getting a good night's sleep

Sleepless nights are not merely frustrating. Chronic difficulties in falling asleep and staying asleep can lead to depression, health problems, and even being accident-prone. Stress at work and financial problems top the lists of most polls that survey why people toss and turn instead of getting a good night's sleep.

dear diva

"I can't seem to fall asleep, and I feel exhausted and anxious all day long. When my head hits the pillow, all of my problems instantly rush to my head and I can't relax. It seems like it gets worse the older I get. How can I get a good night's sleep?"

secrets from the de-stress diva

If you worry over losing sleep, this only adds to the accumulated stress from work, family problems, or finances that keeps you awake in the first place. Short-term insomnia lasts from a few nights to a few weeks. You can take the following proactive steps to get a better night's sleep. If you still have insomnia after a month, call a doctor.

1. **Don't exercise within three hours before bedtime,** because you want your energy level to be down, not up.

2. **Avoid stimulants.** Don't consume caffeine after noon, and avoid alcohol, smoking, sugar, and chocolate, especially before bedtime.

3. **Create a Sleep Comfort Zone.** Your Sleep Comfort Zone should be cool. (Studies suggest that the optimum temperature is about 65 degrees Fahrenheit.) Create a Sleep Comfort Zone in a dark and quiet room, turning off all electronic devices. If you have a bedside clock that you can hear ticking, buy another clock. Don't work, eat, watch television, or read in bed.

4. **Drink fewer liquids** at night to minimize trips to the bathroom.

5. **Sleep only at bedtime.** Trying to catch up on sleep during the afternoon with a long nap will only disrupt your goal of achieving a normal sleep cycle.

6. **Make the bedroom a No Worry Zone.** Keep your mind free from worries at night by setting a specific time during the day to concentrate on worrying and to write your worries in a journal or on a piece of paper. Before you go to bed, say out loud, "I send all of my worries upward and let them go, just like a helium balloon."

7. **Divert yourself.** If you can't fall asleep after fifteen minutes, leave the bedroom and do something relaxing (take a bath, read a book, write, or do a few simple stretching exercises). Instead of tossing and turning because you can't fall asleep, you are diverting your attention to a pleasant activity. After twenty or thirty minutes, go back to the bedroom. If that doesn't work, repeat this exercise.

Have a Cup of Tea

Herbal teas have been used for hundreds of years to relax people into having a good night's sleep. A cup of hot tea warms and soothes the body. Chamomile tea is a favorite. Other calming herbal teas can contain passion flower, skullcap, or valerian.

About Snoring

As many as half of all adults snore occasionally, and about 25 percent of us snore regularly.

- Since being overweight can lead to snoring, exercise every day and eat nutritious foods to maintain a healthy weight.
- Avoid heavy meals and alcohol before bedtime.
- Let the person who doesn't snore fall asleep first.
- Sleep on your side instead of on your back.

Milk Is Calming

Combine warm milk, honey, and a sprinkle of cinnamon. Since milk contains tryptophan, it may help to promote sleep.

Music

When I had difficulty sleeping several years ago, I found soothing music that helped me fall asleep. Every night I fell asleep at the same section of the music!

Foods

To stabilize moods and alleviate stress, make sure that you get enough of the amino acid tryptophan in your diet. It produces serotonin, which regulates the mechanisms of normal sleep. Foods that are high in tryptophan include bananas, fish, dates, milk, peanuts, and turkey.

Homeopathy

Dr. Mindy Boxer, a doctor of homeopathy, said that this works for an overactive mind.

Coffea Cruda 30X or 15C

Take one dose an hour before dinner and another dose a half hour before bedtime. It will help calm the nervous system.

> daily aspiration   "I sleep peacefully."

eating and being well

47 eat well and feel well

Sure, diets can be stressful, but did you know that stress can also sabotage your diet? A new study by researchers at Georgetown University in the United States and the Garvan Institute of Medical Research in Australia reported a direct link between chronic stress and obesity. Everyone knows that the best diet is low in fats and sugars and has plentiful fruits, vegetables, and healthy proteins. So why are obesity rates skyrocketing among the young and the old in America, and what can you do about it?

dear diva

"I don't have the time or the money to prepare exotic meals with all of the healthy ingredients that cost so much at the local health food store. But I don't like what I see in the mirror, either. How can I eat healthier?"

secrets from the de-stress diva

1. **Ditch the "d" word.** The word *diet* is a negative term that implies not being able to eat what you want. No wonder most diets fail; the stress they cause literally makes you fatter! Replace the word *diet* with the words *healthy eating*. That's a positive phrase.

2. **Eat what you want. But in small portions.** If everyone else is eating pizza, your healthy eating plan can allow you to have one small piece. If you crave chocolate, eat a bite instead of a calorie-laden bar. Think in small bites instead of bingeing, and you'll eliminate the stress that comes with total denial.

3. **Take a multivitamin.** Often, you are hungry because your body craves nutrients. The daily stress of your fast-paced world at home and at work can drain your body of the nutrients it needs. The best way to get your vitamins is naturally through the foods you eat, but to be on the safe side, take a daily multivitamin.

4. **Don't skip breakfast.** Skipping breakfast sets you up for feeling fatigued and stressed out by mid-morning and makes you ravenous at lunch. Eat a healthy breakfast with protein to make

yourself feel fuller and keep up your energy levels. If you don't have time to make breakfast, hard boil eggs the night before. Have one or two hard-boiled eggs for breakfast, and make egg salad for lunch or dinner. How easy is that?

5. **Snack away!** Healthy snacks will keep you energized and focused throughout the day and will prevent you from overeating at lunch or dinner. Great snack ideas are a piece of fruit, a hard-boiled egg, or a handful of unsalted nuts. Keep small portions with you at all times to avoid being tempted to reach for unhealthy snacks.

6. **Exercise.** Exercise relieves stress and also produces endorphins, the stress-busting hormones, which can stop you from grabbing fattening comfort foods when you feel stressed.

7. **Drink healthy.** Drink a large glass of water before you eat so that you will feel fuller and won't reach for extra portions. It will also help you digest your food. Caffeinated drinks and alcohol can actually make you feel thirstier, so stick to water.

8. **Don't eat late at night.** Brush your teeth immediately after dinner, and close the kitchen door. Eating late at night can cause insomnia, which will increase your stress levels the next day. Late-night eating can also result in excess weight gain because your body doesn't get a chance to burn off those extra calories before you go to sleep.

Fast, Healthy, Stress-Free Snacks

Healthy snacks will keep your energy level high and will prevent hunger between meals. The goal is to get your snacks ready in advance so that you won't be tempted to visit the vending machine or take extra portions at lunch or dinner. Here are a few snacks that are fast, easy, and inexpensive.

1. Core and cut an apple into slices, and put it in a small sandwich bag to tuck into your purse or desk drawer. You can add lemon juice to keep it from turning brown.

2. Peel an orange and eat it, section by section, when you feel hungry between meals. An orange contains many fewer calories than a large glass of orange juice, and the process of peeling it will divert your attention away from a stressful situation for a minute or two.

3. Hard-boil an egg to peel and eat later for a high-protein snack. Sprinkle it with a dash of a spicy salt substitute to add zest.

4. Nuts are nutritious but can pack on the calories. Premeasure eight to ten nuts, and put these small portions in plastic sandwich bags to keep yourself from eating more than half a handful at a time.

5. Decorate your yogurt. Reward yourself with what you crave by opening up a single serving of low-fat yogurt, adding a drizzle of chocolate or fresh fruit preserves, and resealing it for a snack later. Yes, you can have your chocolate and eat healthily, too.

6. Have a cup of broth. Substitute a cup of no-fat broth for that afternoon cup of coffee or tea. You'll feel fuller. Plus, a steaming cup of broth is considered comfort food, too, to help you get through a high-stress afternoon.

For more healthy snack ideas, check out www.destressdiva.com/healthysnacks.

Herbs

Adding fresh or dried herbs is a wonderful way to impart interesting flavors to plain and ordinary dishes. Each herb has its own distinct flavor and is healthy as well. Herbs are easy to grow in your garden, on your patio or rooftop, or inside your home with good lighting.

- Make a bouquet of herbs to flavor stews, casseroles, and soups. Use regular string without any coloring to tie together a fresh bay leaf and a sprig of parsley and thyme.

- Freeze fresh herbs because freezing preserves their natural flavor. Store them in tablespoon-size amounts in an ice cube tray. Pour water into the tray to cover the chopped herbs and then freeze. Add the ice cubes to soup stock while it's cooking, and stir.

---

daily aspiration "I eat healthy meals every day."

48 vitamins

The healthiest way to get your vitamins is naturally, through the foods you eat. But you may not have time to get all of the nutrients you need by eating nourishing meals every day. In addition, high-stress days can sabotage your healthy eating habits by draining your body of nutrients so it is easy to become deficient in these. Therefore, the second-best way to get adequate nutrition is to take a multivitamin. Be careful, however, not to take such high doses of any vitamin that it damages your health.

dear diva

"I've been to vitamin stores, and I feel overwhelmed, which is ironic, since the reason I walked into the store in the first place was to find vitamins that would make me feel less stressed. There are so many hundreds of vitamins and supplements to choose from. I don't know where to turn. How can I find the vitamins that will make me feel less stressed and healthier?"

secrets from the de-stress diva

You can avoid becoming confused by ignoring the advertising gimmicks and focusing on what's right for your health. First, look for the USP-DSVP seal of approval, which is issued by the U.S. Pharmacopoeia Dietary Supplement Validation Program. The seal indicates USP's assurance that the vitamin's manufacturer has complied with certain standards of production.

In spite of what the manufacturer may claim, a 2007 study by Harvard medical researchers advises that multivitamin and multimineral supplements ought not to exceed 150 percent of the recommended daily value (DV on the bottle) for any nutrient. In fact, for trace minerals, such as iron, fluoride, and zinc, it's safest not to exceed the DV at all, according to the Harvard study.

The ABCs of Anti-Stress Vitamins

1. **A for Avoiding Stress!** Vitamin A is a powerful antioxidant that helps to relieve stress and also strengthens your

immune system. It's a powerful aid for your vision, as well. Milk, eggs, dark green or orange vegetables, and fruits are high in vitamin A.

2. **B for Busting through Fatigue.** Vitamins B_{12} and B_6 energize you to overcome the fatigue results from stress and are also general stress-relief vitamins. B vitamins boost your metabolism and act almost like serotonin to soothe your nerves. A member of the vitamin B family called pantothenic acid, along with vitamin C, helps to remove the stress hormone cortisol and other toxins from your body.

3. **C for Coping.** Vitamin C is a powerful, stress-busting antioxidant that also helps your body to dissolve cortisol. Cooking can destroy vitamin C, so eat your tomatoes, citrus fruits, and green vegetables uncooked.

Choosing Vitamins (and Supplements) the Smart Way

With so many brand names and bottles, it can be confusing to choose the right vitamin at the right price. Here is some sensible advice, compliments of the Mayo Clinic:

- **Check the label.** Read labels carefully to determine the active ingredient and the level of nutrient in each serving.
- **Calcium.** Each multivitamin tablet or capsule would be enormous if it contained enough calcium to cover 100 percent of the daily requirement. For that reason, and especially if you are a woman, an additional calcium supplement might be needed if you are not drinking enough nonfat milk or eating other foods with high levels of naturally occurring calcium.
- **Look for "USP" on the label.** This tells you that the vitamin or the supplement has undergone strict testing for strength, purity, disintegration, and dissolution according to standards established by the U.S. Pharmacopeia.
- **Look for expiration dates.** Dietary supplements can lose potency over time, especially if you live in a hot, humid climate. Discard expired vitamins and supplements. Store your vitamins and supplements in a cool, dry place.

Quercetin

Quercetin is a flavonoid that is found naturally in apples, onions, and broccoli. Research has shown that it may help to prevent illness and maintain your mental performance while you are physically stressed.

Vitamins in Food

Beta-carotene is a precursor to vitamin A. It is converted into vitamin A by the body.

- Beta-carotene is found in orange veggies, orange fruits, and tomatoes.

Vitamin B complex is made up of thiamine (B_1), riboflavin (B_2), pyridoxine (B_6), cobalamin (B_{12}), niacin, and pantothenic acid. These vitamins are necessary for your body to metabolize carbohydrates, fats, and proteins. They help the nervous system function, increase energy, and help to lower stress levels. They also promote healthy blood and aid in the growth of skin and nails.

- B-complex vitamins are found in nutritional yeast, wheat germ, whole grains, whole-wheat flour, liver, lean meat, cheese, milk, chicken, leafy green veggies, dried beans, peas, and nuts.

Folate is considered a brain food. It helps with red blood cell formation and strengthens immunity.

- Folate is contained in cooked beans or peas, oranges, dark-green leafy veggies, nutritional yeast, brown rice, lentils, salmon, whole wheat, and peanuts.

(Resource: *The De-Stress Diva in the Kitchen*, Ruth Klein, www.destressdiva.com)

daily aspiration   "I eat nutritious vegetables every day."

49 what do *you* want to eat for dinner?

Americans are working longer hours, and children spend more time each day in school than in any previous generation. Who has time for healthy eating? The problem is that obesity has become an epidemic, thanks to poor eating habits and our sedentary lifestyles.

Being overweight can lead to diabetes, coronary heart disease, high cholesterol, stroke, hypertension, insomnia, depression and other psychological disorders, stress incontinence, and increased mortality. De-stressing everyday meals can keep you and your family healthy with a relaxed approach to cooking that focuses on nutritious ingredients.

dear diva

"I'm not aiming to be the next Top Chef. I just want to prepare healthy, everyday meals my family will enjoy, without the stress and the expense. How can I make time to prepare healthy meals every day?"

secrets from the de-stress diva

1. **Hire Chef Crockpot.** Using a crockpot is an inexpensive and easy way to prepare healthy meals in the morning that will be ready by dinnertime. These slow cookers roast meats and vegetables for six to eight hours, producing tender, tasty meals with fewer calories and less mess than when you fry foods on a stovetop.

2. **Hire Chef George.** As in the George Foreman grill (or any variation of the indoor electric grill). These grills are built to drain unwanted fats and oils into an easy-to-clean drip pan, and most foods take only five to fifteen minutes or less to grill. You can combine meats and vegetables, or grill only vegetables.

3. **Stock your cupboard the healthy way.** If you don't keep unhealthy foods around the kitchen, you won't reach for them when you cook. Buy healthy staples such as nonfat chicken or vegetable broth and plenty of seasonings. Choose fresh vegetables over canned or

frozen. Choose sweet potatoes over plain potatoes for the extra vitamins. Choose organic over nonorganic foods to avoid long-term threats to your health from chemical additives. An organically grown chicken might cost twice as much, but it will taste better and be healthier for you. Aren't you worth it?

4. **Integrate.** Combine other activities with your kitchen chores to make cooking and cleaning up less stressful. Invite your children to discuss their day and homework challenges with you while you chop, cook, and clean. Practice deep breathing and stretching exercises while you reach for ingredients, plates, and silverware. Listen to soothing music or tapes that teach you a foreign language while you work. Integrating important or enjoyable activities into cooking can double the rewards of preparing and serving healthy meals.

5. **De-stress your table.** Ban negative conversations at the table. If an unpleasant topic arises, say, "Let's talk about that after the meal." Ask everyone at your table to share a pleasant memory from the day or from the previous month or year. Smiling is as contagious as yawning, so smile while you are at the table. Make your table cheerful with a vase of fresh flowers or a bowl of fruit. On gloomy days, use silly paper napkins. People digest their food better in a calm and loving environment.

6. **Have fresh water at the table.** Keep pitchers of water on the table to encourage your family or friends to drink plenty of refreshing water with their meals. It's a healthy, zero-calorie substitute for sugary or caffeinated drinks. Dress up your pitcher of water with thin slices of lime or lemon (or a dash of crushed mint) to make water an attractive treat.

7. **Plan ahead for the next healthy meal.** Invite family members to contribute to the next meal, using ingredients on hand. Ask younger family members to band together to create a fun recipe. Make meals a joyous group endeavor by letting the kids or your friends take over your kitchen one day a week.

Slow Cooker and Indoor Grilling Recipes

GRILLED HALIBUT

Preparation time: 35 minutes
Cooking time: 10 minutes

Serves 4

3 tablespoons fresh ginger, minced
1 clove garlic, minced
1 bunch scallions, chopped
¼ cup tamari or soy sauce

3 tablespoons dry sherry
1 tablespoon toasted sesame oil
4 6-ounce halibut fillets, rinsed

1. Mix all of the ingredients except the halibut in a blender.
2. Pour the mixture over the fish and marinate it for 30 minutes.
3. Grill the fish on an indoor counter grill for 5 minutes on each side.
4. This recipe is easy, fast, and delicious!

De-Stress Diva's note: Try this with chicken pieces as well.

CHICKEN WITH SALSA

Preparation time: 5 minutes
Cooking time on low: 4–6 hours
Cooking time on high: 1½–3 hours

Serves 4–6

1 onion, chopped
1 tablespoon extra virgin olive oil
4 pounds chicken pieces, beef, or
   vegetarian "meat"
2 fresh carrots, sliced

1 stalk celery, chopped
⅛ cup barley
16-ounce jar of your favorite salsa
½ cup water or stock

1. Sauté the onion in olive oil for 3 to 4 minutes and add the chicken, beef, or vegetarian "meat."
2. Sear the chicken on both sides for a few minutes on each side.
3. Place the veggies and the barley in a slow cooker. Add the sautéed onions and the chicken to the cooker over the veggies.
4. Top off everything with the entire jar of salsa and the water.
5. Cook the dish in the slow cooker on the low setting for 4–6 hours or on the high setting for 1½–3 hours.

De-Stress Diva's note: Try mango or peach salsa for a tasty variation.

FAVORITE CHILI

Preparation time: 10 minutes
Cooking time on low : 4–6 hours
Cooking time on high: 1½ hours

Serves 4–6

1½ pounds ground beef
16 ounces whole tomatoes, diced
15 ounces stewed tomatoes

15 ounces each kidney beans, lentils, and garbanzo beans

1. Combine all of the ingredients in a slow cooker, with the veggies at the bottom.
2. Cook for 4–6 hours on the low setting or 1½ hours on the high setting.

> **daily aspiration**
> "I am preparing quick, healthy meals."

50 grocery shopping made easy

Even the way that men and women shop for groceries has become the subject of scientific studies. A team of researchers from Yale University and the University of California at Santa Barbara discovered that men and women shop differently. When it comes to grocery stores, women are just as skilled as men at navigating the aisles. In fact, men, who are supposed to be better at spatial problems (such as reading maps), scored slightly lower than women when navigating grocery store aisles to find foods they had previously purchased. Alas, women were more adept at finding high-calorie foods, such as doughnuts, than the male subjects were. The memory for high-calorie foods, such as honey and avocados, was as much as four times as accurate as the memory for low-calorie foods, the researchers reported. Fortunately, we all are individuals, and we all have the same capacity to be smart about grocery shopping, however we navigate the aisles.

dear diva

"I'm always in such a hurry and usually starving, too, when I stop at the grocery store on the way home from work. It's stressful, knowing that this is one more chore I have to hurry through, and I always end up with overpriced food that goes to waste. How can I make grocery shopping more productive?"

secrets from the de-stress diva

There's an art and a profit motive to stocking grocery store shelves that can work against the shopper who is looking for healthier foods at competitive prices. For example, "island displays" in the middle of the store often promote higher-priced, usually higher-calorie foods. Ditto for end-of-the-aisle displays. A handy rule of thumb is this: fresh staples such as milk, fruits, vegetables, and meats are usually located at the back or along the sides of the store. Junk foods and nonstaples are usually in the middle aisles. The moral is: shop at the perimeters.

Ten Smart Grocery Shopping Tips

1. **Do your homework.** Check your supplies before you go to the store to avoid buying what you already have. Make a list of what you need and stick to it.

2. **Eat before you go.** Hungry shoppers will be more inclined to stock up on fresh-baked breads and other items they might not need. Even if you must stop at a grocery store on the way home from work or school, have a little snack first. Never shop while hungry.

3. **Buy locally grown foods.** They're fresher and usually less chemical-laden, and you're doing your part to grow your local economy and save the environment.

4. **Have fun.** Go ahead. Set aside $1 or $3 for an impulse buy, but don't exceed your limit. Your impulse buy will be your reward for shopping, but make sure that it's a reasonably priced reward.

5. **Comparison shop.** If the store-brand item has the same ingredients as the brand name item, try the generic version. You'll save money and that's smart!

6. **Use coupons.** You don't have to become a coupon fanatic to benefit from using coupons on items that you know you'll use. Many companies now allow you to download coupons off the Internet for some items. Saving even a few cents off each trip can quickly add up. Go to www.coupons.com for a head start!

7. **Avoid trips to the convenience store.** Because it is convenient, it charges higher prices, especially for staples.

Go back to number 1 and do your homework. Make sure that you shop before you entirely run out of a staple.

8. **Shop alone.** You're on a mission, not a family cruise. You'll avoid the stress of babysitting the contents of your cart to see what's been added that you don't need if you go alone and stick to your list. Have your family help you unload, not load up.

9. **Buy "on sale" staples** if they can be wrapped and frozen for later use. You'll save money. If the price is cheaper per ounce, you can carefully wrap and store portions to use over time.

10. **Avoid "eye-level" shopping.** Manufacturers essentially pay for shelf space, and the most enviable is at eye level. Look at the shelf at eye level. Now look both up and below for better prices.

Discount and Outlet Stores

They call them "big box" stores because superstores such as Costco and Sam's Club offer bargains based on large quantities. But first ask yourself, do you have space to store fifty rolls of toilet paper? Often, you can use coupons to get similar deals for smaller amounts at "regular-size" stores if you're not shopping for a family of twenty. Bakery outlets can offer significant savings on breads that you can freeze for later use; however, most bakery outlets stock as many cakes and doughnuts as they do whole-wheat bread products. Ask yourself, is it cheaper to save $1 on cupcakes each week when you will end up spending $50 on a new pair of pants in a bigger size?

There are times when you just get bored with grocery shopping because you feel as if you always get the same foods and products. To add a little adventure to your shopping trips, try to buy one new product and/or one new fresh fruit or veggie each time. Ask the grocer how to prepare it or go online to find out.

Farmers' Markets

I happen to love farmers' markets because of the energy of the people and the growers, the excitement about new veggies or fruits that are in season and ready to eat, and the delicious samples. Here are five more reasons to shop at your local farmers' market:

1. **Freshness.** The fruits and the veggies have stayed on the trees and the vines longer than conventional store-bought produce has (which allows the sun to sweeten the produce naturally), and you'll find they're at their peak time for quality and ripeness.
2. **Variety.** I am always amazed at the new varieties or very old varieties that are now grown.
3. **Health.** I stay in the "organic" section of the farmer's market, which is growing larger all the time. I love knowing that my produce is not covered with pesticides and herbicides.
4. **Environment.** Local farmers' markets save on fuel and other costs that are incurred by produce grown thousands of miles away from where you live. Don't forget to bring your own shopping bags.
5. **Community.** Buying locally keeps the people, the jobs, and the money local as well.

Fall Harvest

Most of us learned while growing up that there is an abundance of delicious fresh fruits during the summer. When we get busy in the fall, either going back to school or gearing up to work on projects for the third quarter, we may forget about all of the healthful bounty that we can buy when grocery shopping.

Apples. You can find apples at the height of their season from August to October; 2,500-plus apple varieties are grown in the United States.

Almonds. Almonds are a very healthy snack to take to work or put in the children's lunch boxes. They're great for baking as well.

Cinnamon. Studies have found a major link between cinnamon and good health. Try sprinkling cinnamon on your fancy coffee drinks or steep a cinnamon stick in a cup of tea or hot apple cider for a change of taste in your beverage.

Pumpkin (or other squash). I had my first piece of pumpkin pie in my twenties. Since then I have made countless pies.

But I also use acorn squash in recipes, which is delicious and nutritious. You'll find some wonderful recipes using acorn squash on my Web site, www.destressdiva.com. You will need to type in your name, your e-mail address, and the code DSDW to access the information.

ACORN SQUASH WITH SPINACH AND CHEESE

Preparation time: 10 minutes
Baking time: 50 minutes

Serves 6–8

4 acorn squash (or another variety)
Sea salt and black pepper to taste
2 cloves garlic, crushed
2 teaspoons olive oil

8 ounces fresh baby spinach
6 ounces Gorgonzola cheese, crumbled

1. Preheat the oven to 375 degrees F.
2. Cut the tops off the squash and scoop out the seeds.
3. Season the squash with salt and pepper. Bake them with the cut sides down in a roasting pan for 35 minutes.
4. Sauté the garlic in the olive oil and add the fresh spinach until it's just wilted. Season it with salt and pepper.
5. Fill the squash cavities with the spinach mixture, top each one with the cheese, and bake them until the cheese melts, about 7 minutes.

Reframe Your Grocery-Shopping Experience

You may want to categorize grocery shopping as a tedious chore, but reframe the way you think about it. Tell yourself:

"I have the opportunity to role-model healthy food choices for my children."

"I have the money to purchase food that my family enjoys."

"I am taking the time to keep myself and my family healthy and nourished with good food."

daily aspiration   "I am grateful to be able to buy good food for myself and my family."

51 *diet* is a four-letter word

Every year, the latest, hottest dieting fads capture headlines and fill the airwaves with infomercials claiming to have the secret to the fastest, easiest way to lose weight. Physicians shake their heads, but their commonsense advice is often drowned out by all the hoopla.

The National Institute on Aging studied societies around the world to find the real "secret" to living a long, healthy life. What the diverse communities of long-living people had in common was a sensible diet, an active lifestyle, and positive attitudes. People in these communities eat fresh foods in moderation, have strong family or social support systems, and get plenty of exercise.

dear diva

"I've been on all of those so-called yo-yo diets, and my weight goes up and down but never stays down. I want to be healthier, but I also need to get this weight off fast. I feel so bad about myself. How can I lose weight when I've tried it before, and it hasn't worked?"

secrets from the de-stress diva

1. **Erase the word *diet* from your vocabulary.** The word *diet* carries too many negative connotations of deprivation and failure, as in, "I must starve myself and eat foods I hate," and "I'm so fat, everyone belittles me by saying I must go on a diet, as if I didn't already know that." So don't think *diet*; think *healthy lifestyle*. Vow to adopt a healthier lifestyle that includes better nutrition, more exercise, and a positive attitude, and you'll reach your goals.

2. **Set realistic goals.** Losing 10 pounds a week is not only unrealistic, it's unhealthy and can produce the yo-yo dieting effect, where rapid weight loss is followed by rapid weight gain, severely damaging your overall health. Stay away from fad diets that suggest you can lose weight fast without eating sensibly or exercising. Those quick weight-loss schemes do not work. Period. Choose a goal you can achieve, such as losing 1 to 2 pounds each week

while you also tone your body with exercise in order to look and feel better.

3. **Don't skip meals.** Instead, reduce the portion size. Research confirms that people who eat regular meals maintain a healthier weight than do those who overeat, skip meals, or snack all day long. Eat foods that are low in fat and refined sugars, and eat smaller portions if you are overweight. Ban all junk food from your diet *and your home*. It's that simple.

4. **Exercise.** Exercise is your friend. Not only does exercise help you maintain a healthy lifestyle and a positive self-image, but it is also a perfect time to brainstorm. Exercise boosts your metabolism so that it burns more calories, even when you are resting. Resolve to exercise at least twenty to thirty minutes a day, not as a quick-fix way to lose weight but as a lifetime habit.

5. **Track your habits.** Keep a healthy lifestyle journal. Write down what you have accomplished and what your intentions are for the next day. If you have poor eating habits, it's an eye-opener to "see" those habits spelled out on a piece of paper. Use your self-knowledge to adjust your eating and exercise habits accordingly.

6. **Don't punish yourself; reward yourself.** Don't punish yourself if you start and fail to maintain a healthy lifestyle. Just vow to do better the next day. Changing your lifestyle is not simple or easy, so forgive yourself often. You may reward yourself by occasionally indulging in your favorite food. You can have a half-cup of low-fat ice cream to keep from feeling deprived; however, vow to walk to the ice cream parlor or to eat a smaller meal the next day to make up for your indulgence.

Boosting Your Endorphins

The de-stress way to lose weight is to boost your body's production of endorphins, which serve to decrease your appetite, reduce stress, block pain, and create a feeling of euphoria that is often called the "runner's high." The way to increase your body's endorphins is free and easy: it's called exercise! The more you exercise, the more sensitive you are to the endorphins in your body, which means that you feel even better exercising after you've been working out regularly over a long period of time.

It's a win-win situation that is your body's way of helping you to reach your healthier lifestyle goals.

Eliminate Temptations

Everywhere you go, you are tempted by junk food ads, dessert carts, and foods that are rich in taste but also, alas, in calories. New "one-touch" technologies make it easier for you to go through life without ever having to get out of your chair. But you have the power to control your environment by eliminating junk food from your cupboards and your vocabulary. You can thwart technology by hiding your remote control devices and taking frequent exercise breaks away from your computer, cell phone, DVD player, TV set, and video game machine. You can share your goals with others and ask for their support to help you avoid temptations. Get a nutrition buddy to share recipes and meals. Get an exercise buddy to take weekly or daily walks or trips to the gym.

Visualize Yourself as Healthy

In your journal, you may want to write something like this: "I am healthy and look slim in my clothes." Say it out loud; then visualize it. You are telling your subconscious that you already have achieved your goals, which creates a powerful impetus to consciously make your vision a reality. Each day, reaffirm your vision to build confidence as you develop and maintain your healthier lifestyle.

> daily aspiration "I look svelte and sexy."

pain: when it really hurts

52 when it's that time of the month again

Premenstrual syndrome, or PMS, can produce symptoms that are mild to severe, ranging from swollen breasts, mood swings, and odd food cravings, to fatigue, irritability, and anger during the days before menstruation. Researchers at the Mayo Clinic report that as many as 75 percent of menstruating women experience at least some form of PMS. Women in their twenties to early forties tend to suffer more. There is help.

dear diva

"PMS makes me feel bloated, and I suffer from the worst cramps. I don't want to get out of bed, much less go to work, and I snap at my coworkers because of my mood swings. How can I survive PMS, stay productive, and live a happy life?"

secrets from the de-stress diva

- **Watch your diet.** Limit salty foods and eat smaller meals to reduce bloating. Take a daily multivitamin. Avoid caffeine, which can heighten feelings of anxiety.
- **Exercise.** Daily exercise can help energize you to fight off fatigue, not to mention improving your overall health.
- **Breathe.** Practice deep-breathing exercises to calm yourself when you feel stressful. Stress exacerbates PMS symptoms, so get plenty of stress-busting sleep and exercise, and do stretching exercises to relax your muscles. Researchers at the Mayo Clinic recommend keeping a PMS diary for several months to track what triggers your PMS symptoms. This will allow you to plan ahead to prevent PMS symptoms.
- **Ask your physician.** If natural remedies fail, ask your doctor about medicines that can help you through the worst of your PMS symptoms. Nonsteroid anti-inflammatory drugs, or NSAIDs, can ease cramping. You can buy over-the-counter NSAIDs such

as ibuprofen or naproxen sodium at your local drugstore. Oral contraceptives have been used to stabilize hormonal swings. In severe cases, ask your doctor about antidepressants that can be taken for two weeks before menstruation begins, versus daily for traditional users of antidepressants.

Nature's Help

Black cohosh has traditionally been used to alleviate hot flashes in menopausal women, but this same herb can provide help to younger women suffering from PMS by relieving stomach cramps and mood swings, according to some researchers. St. John's Wort can lessen mood swings in women with PMS, as well as provide help to menopausal women. St. John's Wort can interact with some prescribed medicines, however, including contraceptive pills. Always consult your physician before using any herbal medicines. Know, too, that herbal medicines are not regulated or screened for safety, effectiveness, or even contents by the U.S. Food and Drug Administration. This means that a bottle can say black cohosh on the label but can contain anything, even chalk, inside. Go to www.consumerreports.org, which is a nonprofit publication that accepts no funding from herbal remedy makers or any other advertisers, as your trusted source for herbal remedies.

Pamper Yourself

Pamper yourself with long, fragrant baths. Light candles with your favorite scents. Buy a beautiful outfit one size larger that you will relish wearing on those days when your weight fluctuates slightly upward because of bloating caused by PMS. Find a PMS buddy who suffers from PMS symptoms at about the same time of month as you. On these days, instead of suffering alone, plan a pleasurable, relaxing activity you can share, such as a movie night at home or a trip to a favorite restaurant.

Aromatherapy

Here's an idea for a PMS massage or body oil:

10 drops geranium oil

6 drops Roman chamomile oil
3 drops angelica oil
2 drops sweet marjoram oil
Add all of the oils to 2 ounces of vegetable oil.

Evening Primrose

Some women report that evening primrose capsules help to relieve many PMS symptoms.

Food

- Create a high-fiber food plan.
- Keep your blood sugar even by eating several small meals during the day.
- Green leafy vegetables are a good source of potassium and have a diuretic effect, if you suffer from water retention.
- Avoid *raw* cabbage, cauliflower, broccoli, and brussels sprouts. The brassica family of vegetables depresses thyroid function when eaten raw.
- Avoid refined carbohydrates such as cane or beet sugar, corn sweeteners, and white-flour products, as well as certain unrefined carbohydrates that are high in natural sugars, like honey, maple syrup, and dried fruit. Honey, maple syrup and dried fruit *are* good sources for sweetener, but they must be used in moderation.
- Reduce your salt intake.

Homeopathy

Dr. Mindy Boxer suggests these tonics for various symptoms of PMS. For each supplement, she recommends that you take three to four tablets under your tongue, three times a day between meals during the week before your period.

Lash out easily. If you are talkative, lash out easily, have tender breasts, and feel worse first thing in the morning, take Lachesis 30X or 16C.

Depression and irritability. For depression and irritability before your period, accompanied by flatulence and cravings for sweets, especially chocolate, take Lycopodium 30X or 15C.

Sadness and melancholy. For sadness, melancholy, salt cravings, and swollen breasts and ankles, take Natrum Muriaticum 30X or 15C.

Emotionally sensitive. If you cry easily or have irregular periods, tender breasts, or an aversion to greasy foods, take Pulsatilla 30X or 15C.

Emotionally apathetic. If you feel irritable and apathetic or have no interest in sex, take Sepia 30X or 15C. You might also try Sepia if you crave salt, sweets, and sour foods (e.g., vinegar) or feel better after exercise.

daily aspiration
"I embrace my femininity."

53 accidents and injuries

The best medicine, of course, is preventive medicine, but accidental injuries will always occur in life. Plus, the escalating cost of health care can mean spending thousands of dollars for even a simple sprain. For the millions of Americans who have no health insurance, the impact can be devastating. At work, the increasing numbers of back injuries reported each year are linked to the stress of spending longer hours on the job, especially when work involves sitting or standing for hours at a time.

dear diva

"My back hurts, but I can't afford to take time off work, I can't afford the therapy, and I can't handle taking care of my children when I am in so much pain. I don't want to get out of bed. How can I avoid becoming injured?"

secrets from the de-stress diva

Injuries are what we fear the most, especially as we grow older and become more prone to age-related injuries and suffer from longer recovery times. When we are caretakers and our children or aging parents become injured, the stress of tending to our injured dependants can seem overwhelming as we try to juggle this with the other daily tasks in our lives.

1. **Be fit; stay fit.** Excess weight and weak muscles can make people more prone to getting injured. Take a yoga class or buy a yoga video to keep your muscles limber. Lose weight if you are overweight, and maintain a desirable weight. It's not only about looking good; it's preventive medicine to avoid expensive, time-wasting injuries.

2. **Ask for help.** If you become injured, ask for help. Ask relatives or friends to help you with your home or work responsibilities while you recover; outside help will speed the healing process. If you must care for an injured child or parent, ask for help. Now is not the time to play Superwoman.

3. **Be smart.** Don't ignore minor injuries that can become serious. If you feel pain, your body is telling you to stop, pay attention, and do something about it. If you twist your ankle walking home from work, rest and apply ice. Don't walk around on it until it becomes so painful, you must seek medical care. If you drive around with a flat tire, you're not looking at paying less than $100 for a new tire; you're going to spend hundreds of dollars for a new rim. Be sensible, and don't make your injury worse by ignoring it.

Avoiding Back Injuries

Back injuries cost U.S. industry millions of dollars each year in lost productivity and medical expenses. They are a common ailment, especially in this sedentary society, where people perform most white-collar jobs while seated at desks for hours at a time each day. What can you do to avoid back injuries?

- Stand up when the telephone rings and remain standing while you have a phone conversation.
- Every thirty minutes, stand up and stretch your legs and arms.

- Every hour, take a five-minute walk outside, up and down the stairs, or through the office hallways.
- At your desk, sit up straight to avoid straining your back. Slouching when you walk also strains your back. As a bonus, when you sit and stand up straight, you look like you've just lost five pounds.
- When you bend down, bend your knees first to relieve pressure on your back. Let your legs do the work when you bend and lift.
- Women, before you put on those high heels, consider how fashionable you will look taking a tumble and then hobbling around in a cast for a month. Wear low- or flat-heeled shoes to work.

About Stress and Injuries

Researchers at the Mayo Clinic report that stress can cause your muscles to tense, making you more prone to becoming injured. Research also shows that stress can lessen your tolerance for pain. When you feel stressed, breathe, stretch, and take energizing walks. Share your frustrations with friends or write down your worries in your journal. Downshifting your stress level is smart preventive medicine that will help you to avoid injuries at home and on the job.

Mini Mind Vacations

Since stress adversely affects your adrenal glands, your entire hormonal system, your nervous system, and, more specifically, your brain, to name a few areas of your body, it makes sense to go on mini mind vacations.

When you feel your stress mounting, empty your mind of worries and get involved in an activity you enjoy, whether it's meditation, dance, yoga, stretching, running, walking, bicycling, swimming, aerobic exercise, sailing, skiing, surfing, reading, or whatever else you consider fun. Just do it!

Aromatherapy

Inflammation is swelling, which results when fluid from surrounding tissues seeps into the inflamed or damaged area. If it turns blue, red, or purple, you have a bruise, which means there are broken blood vessels at the inflamed site . . . hence, the swelling occurs. This pain alerts you to the fact that you need to take care of the injury and you need to rest that part of your body.

Health practitioners say that there are two good ways to reduce the swelling: you can put ice on the inflamed area or use anti-inflammatory essential oils.

Some oils that reduce the swelling from injuries are:

Juniper
Lavender
Rose
German Chamomile
Geranium

Pineapple Juice

Pineapples are full of bromelain, which is a natural protease (enzyme) that you can use to decrease swelling. I made sure that my children drank a lot of pineapple juice before they had their wisdom teeth taken out, so that the bromelain would reduce the swelling caused by the operation . . . and it worked.

Bruise Easily

Check with your health practitioner first, but you may want to increase your intake of vitamin C, with a supplement that includes bioflavonoids.

daily aspiration   "I will pay attention to any swelling and take care of it."

54 headaches

Stress is the most commonly recognized trigger of headaches, according to the National Headache Foundation. Not only can stress cause headaches; it can worsen an existing headache. Chronic and repeated stress will cause daily or almost-daily tension headaches.

dear diva

"My work gives me a headache, and when I arrive home already stressed out, my children, whom I love very much, give me a bigger headache. I can't focus on my work or my family when I have a headache. What can I do to avoid getting headaches?"

secrets from the de-stress diva

1. **Don't ignore serious pain.** If your tension headache suddenly feels much, much worse or extends beyond a day or two, seek the advice of a physician. Never ignore pain that can be the symptom of a serious illness or injury.

2. **Exercise.** Tight muscles caused by high levels of stress trigger most tension headaches. Regular exercise can keep your muscles relaxed and toned and can help you to stave off headaches. If you feel a headache coming on, take a brief, energizing walk that stretches all of your muscles and *breathe deeply.*

3. **Try yoga.** Yoga is a powerful, holistic tool to help you get rid of or minimize the effects of headaches. Take a class or rent a video to learn how to correctly use these ancient exercises for modern headache relief.

4. **Watch your diet.** Poor diets can cause stress headaches. Don't over-caffeinate your day or smoke or drink more than a glass or two of wine or other alcohol. Time-tested headache-busters include milk, bananas, and relaxing herbal teas.

Yoga

Tension headaches (and 90 percent of simple headaches are tension headaches) can be caused by a stiff neck and shoulders.

Simple yoga exercises can relieve tension, relax muscles, and make headaches go away. With any yoga exercise, do each move slowly, keep your shoulders and neck relaxed, and practice good posture. Here's a simple neck exercise that's recommended by yoga experts at www.abc-of-yoga.com (which also features animated cartoons showing you how each exercise is performed).

- Take a deep breath in and bend your head forward, chin on your chest, and exhale while bringing your head back to the original position.
- Inhale, bend your head to the right while looking forward, and exhale while going back to the original position.
- Inhale and bend your head back slightly. Exhale as you go back to the original position.
- Inhale and bend your head to the left while looking forward. Exhale as you go back to the original position.
- Inhale as you bend forward, with your chin on your chest, moving your head from right to left, then from left to right. Finally, exhale as you move to back to the original position.

Have a Cup of Tea

A cup of hot herbal tea can reduce the anxiety that causes tension headaches. Try teas that contain these ingredients:

- Chamomile is used to calm nerves, alleviate stress, and even help with stomachaches.
- Lavender can be so relaxing that people often have a cup of lavender tea just before bedtime.
- Lemongrass is a fragrant herb that can also get rid of headaches.
- Lemon verbena, too, is a headache-relieving ingredient in some calming teas.

Aromatherapy

Inhale lavender, lemon, or a combination of peppermint and eucalyptus to alleviate your headache. Studies show that you can also use these combinations as a balm to place on your temples.

Massage

Many studies have found that the neck and the shoulders tense up when a person is under stress. Have a friend or a masseuse massage your neck and shoulders to help you de-stress. Make sure you drink a lot of water afterward to help flush out the toxins that were dislodged and moved around during the massage.

Warm Foot Bath

According to reflexology, the various organ systems of your body correspond to particular areas on the soles of your feet. When these areas are massaged, you are benefiting the corresponding area in the body. Similarly, if you relax by soaking your feet, your whole body will benefit.

- Soak your feet in hot water with Epsom salts.
- Read a good book and enjoy this relaxing time.

Reflexology

Take the thumb and the index finger of your right or left hand and position them on the web part of your other hand, with your thumb above the web and your index finger below the web. Press down with your thumb and up with your index finger together, "pinching" the top part of the web in a tight grip. Keep the pressure on this spot for five minutes.

> daily aspiration
> "I breathe in calmness and harmony."

55 aches and pains

Muscle aches and pains are common and can include more than one muscle. According to researchers at the National Institutes of Health, muscle pain can also involve ligaments, tendons, and fascia, the soft tissues that connect muscles, bones, and organs. Stress plays a powerful role in bringing on your aches and pains. Tension makes your muscles cramp, which can cause mild to sharp episodes of pain. Overusing and also underusing your muscles can result in aches and pains, which is why it is so important to change positions often if you stand or sit for long periods of time.

dear diva

"My aches and pains seem to get worse every day, but I don't have time to take off work and rest up, and I don't want to take pills. How can I avoid everyday aches and pains?"

secrets from the de-stress diva

1. **Call your doctor** if your aches and pains are severe. They can be the symptoms of a serious condition. Don't risk your health by trying to "ride out" severe pain.

2. **Change positions.** If you are standing for long periods of time, take breaks to stretch and change positions. Even placing one foot on a ledge or a box a few inches higher than the floor helps to relieve muscle tension. If you are sitting for most of the day, don't! Take frequent breaks to stand and stretch. Take a walk while you are going over your notes for the day. Stand up and move around when you answer the telephone. Flex your fingers and toes in and out, in and out, every hour. Take five-minute walks every hour or two.

3. **Stretch gently.** Gentle stretches can relax cramped, aching muscles. Never stretch to the point where you feel pain.

4. **Massage your aching muscles.** Ah, the power of massage. You can massage your own muscles by gently kneading tight shoulders, legs, or necks. Even better, ask a loved one to pamper you with a gentle massage.

5. **Exercise regularly.** The best way to avoid muscle aches and pains is to tone up those muscles with regular exercise. This will also keep you limber so that you avoid serious injuries.

6. **Get a good night's sleep.** A restorative night's sleep is just as important as exercise in keeping you fit enough to avoid muscle aches and pains. Meditation for even a minute or a few minutes

each day is also a wonderful tool to de-stress your mind and body during the day.

Massage

10 drops cypress essential oil
6 drops sage essential oil
10 drops lemon essential oil
1 ounce sesame oil

Blend the essential oils into the sesame oil and mix well. Use to massage your tired or painful legs.

Aromatherapy

There are essential oils that relax sore and stiff muscles and may reduce some of the pain. In addition to using them on your sore muscles, you can sniff them because they act as emotional relaxants.

A blend for athletes can provide the perfect relief for tired, stiff, and aching muscles. Terri Hicks, an aromatherapist, uses this recipe:

1 ounce carrier oil or lotion
2 drops ginger essential oil
2 drops coriander essential oil
2 drops eucalyptus essential oil
2 drops sweet birch essential oil
2 drops bay essential oil

Mix the oils and apply the blend to sore and tired muscles.

Peppermint essential oil is another favorite for tired, aching muscles. Peppermint oil is also mentally uplifting, to give yourself extra encouragement to make it to the gym. Using either 1 ounce of carrier oil or 1 ounce of distilled water, add 10 drops of peppermint. Apply the mixture to the areas of your body that need it. Peppermint is an excellent oil to help reduce inflammation, too.

daily aspiration   "I am free of pain."

de-stress your relationships

56 i love my children ... most of the time

Parenting can be difficult, especially with all of the other demands on your time. In fact, more than 80 percent of parents believe that being a parent is harder today than it used to be, according to a study by the Families and Work Institute in Washington, D.C. A full 100 percent of the parents surveyed said that they had less time to spend with their family than they would like. Parents everywhere, from all cultural, racial, religious, and social backgrounds, want the same things for their children: health, growth, happiness, and plenty of opportunities for success when the children are old enough to leave the nest. Most parents know that having the time to show their children that they care is the key to children recognizing and taking advantage of those opportunities.

dear diva

"My children crave my attention. Their demanding behavior gives me a headache. How can I spend more valuable time with my children?"

secrets from the de-stress diva

Children will do whatever they think is necessary to receive the attention they want—and, I might add, *deserve*—from their parents and other loved ones. Even if their behavior gets them in trouble, at least someone has paid attention to them.

How would you describe your perfect day with your child? Answer this for each child, as each one has different needs and interests.

It is important to do the following things often. Just as you eat several meals a day, every day, you need to be present and attentive with your children several times a day as well. Food nourishes children's bodies, and positive attention nourishes their hearts.

WITH GIRLS

Every evening, I asked my daughter whether she would like to have a "tea party" with me. She almost always said yes. It was our code for spending quality time together. So often, I was incredibly tired, but I knew that ten or fifteen minutes of private time with my daughter would eliminate her acting out. We had tea parties from the time that she was in grammar school through to the present, and she is currently a young adult. I simply made herbal teas, and we sat at the kitchen table sipping it. I let her talk and talk. The amazing thing about children is that they will talk if they know you care and are listening.

WITH BOYS

My two boys enjoyed playing ball, any type of ball, so I asked them whether they wanted to play "football." That was our code for throwing the ball to one another. I found that as my boys became older, they did not enjoy the tea parties as much. My younger one did not like tea at all, and I couldn't get him to join in. When these boys had a ball in their hands, however, they would talk nonstop.

Bach Flower Essences

Holly is a good flower essence for children who are jealous of their siblings and may crave extra attention from their parents.

Acupressure

To help relieve a tension headache, place your right index finger-tip in the hollow at the right side of the base of your skull, then place your left index finger one finger-width above your eyebrow, lined up with your pupil. Apply a gentle but firm pressure for two minutes, breathing deeply the whole time. Switch sides, and repeat with your other eyebrow.

Reflexology

Apply lavender essential oil to your temples. Then:

1. Apply pressure to the inside of the base of the big toe three times for ten seconds each time.
2. Massage your temples for five minutes. Breathe deeply.

3. Do ten neck rolls. Pull your ear lobes for five seconds. Rub all around your ear shells.

4. Hold your hand open, palm down, and massage the flesh between your thumb and forefinger with your other hand. The headache should begin to fade.

57 family time can be relaxing

Sitting down with your family or family of friends for a healthy, happy, stress-free meal can be a joyous occasion. Too few busy families make time for this disappearing tradition. A 2005 study by researchers at the University of Minnesota on adolescent eating behaviors found that those who regularly ate structured meals with their families in a congenial atmosphere suffered dramatically fewer eating disorders than did children who seldom dined with their families. "Making family meals a priority, in spite of scheduling difficulties, emerged as the most consistent protective factor for disordered eating," the study's authors wrote in the *Journal of Adolescent Health* following publication of the report.

The goal is to create a time in your schedule for sit-down meals and vow to keep conversations positive. These factors are more important than whether the meals are homemade or fast-food fare, the researchers reported. According to the National Center on Addiction and Substance Abuse (CASA), children who eat meals with their families are more likely to eat healthier meals. CASA reports that teenagers who enjoy frequent family dinners are also less likely than other teens to have sex at younger ages, get into fights, become severely depressed, or be suspended from school.

dear diva

"I don't know any quick, easy, and nutritious meals to make for dinner. I'm so tired at the end of the day."

secrets from the de-stress diva

The family dinner table creates an opportunity for open communications. You can plan the next day's dinner with your family, ask those at the table to share their favorite part of the day, and learn about one another's likes and dislikes.

There is ample evidence that the benefits far outweigh the extra effort involved in scheduling a minimum of three family meals every week. Cutting back on your outside obligations allows you to make more time to enjoy the company of family and friends. And what better place than at the table? With a little planning, you can come home from a full day away from the house and smell the aroma of a wonderful meal cooking in your kitchen. Think of preparing dinner and enjoying it with your family or friends as a special gift you give to yourself . . . the gift of quality time to enjoy the people you love. If it's important enough to you, you'll make it work.

Slow cookers are a great time saver. There are so many wonderful slow cooker dinners that you can quickly and easily start before you leave the house in the morning, then come home to a dinner made by your "wife." Yes, that is how I refer to the slow cooker: as my "wife." In fact, forget the diamonds; a working woman's best friend is either a slow cooker or an indoor grill. Let's look at some fast, easy slow cooker meals you can make in the morning, as well as healthy grilled meals you can make within thirty minutes.

Slow Cooker Dinner Recipe

This is so easy. Add a fresh salad and voilà!

1. Place some chicken or meat in a slow cooker.
2. Pour a jar of salsa over the meat.
3. Cook it on low for six hours or on high for three hours.

Indoor Grill Recipe

This will take you less than twenty minutes for the entire dinner.

1. Place chicken pieces, meat, or fish on the grill and cook for seven minutes on each side.
2. Remove the chicken and add fresh veggies, even the tough ones like green beans, sliced eggplant, and sliced potatoes,

and grill the veggies in the juice from the chicken or the meat, and sprinkle on some wheat-free tamari sauce.

If you would like some more suggestions for thirty-minute dinners that you can make, please check out the quick, healthy, and easy recipes at www.destressdiva.com/recipes, www.kids health.org, and www.familyeducation.com.

Herbs

Ginseng may benefit your health in so many ways, as has been proved by its five-thousand-year track record. The herb is reported to improve coordination and reaction time, increase energy, help the body to fight off infections, normalize "bad" (LDL) cholesterol and blood-sugar levels, regulate hormones, and improve memory and other cognitive functions. Ask your health professional whether this is a good herb for you.

Yoga

Mini yoga literally takes only a minute to do. There are two parts to each yoga exercise: one is the actual movement and the other is your mind-set. Think relaxing thoughts and slowly roll your shoulders forward four times, then roll them gently back four times. Make sure that you're sitting up straight with your feet pressed to the floor and that your back is straight, without any curving.

Dinner Time

Making the dinner hour enjoyable and nonstressful is important for any family. Plus, the more pleasurable dinner time becomes, the more often your family will want to participate.

A few ideas to remember when you're having dinner with the family:

- The television is *off*.
- Cell phones are *off* or on *silent*.
- Landlines do *not* get answered; the same goes for voice mail and the answering machine.

- This is the time to be positive and *not* criticize anyone at the table.
- Dinner is *not* the time to blame or shame anyone at the table.

If you follow these simple guidelines, everyone will benefit.

Family Night

1. Set aside one night a week, preferably the same night each week, as a time when everyone in the family looks forward to being together, whether it's for an hour or four hours.
2. Stick to the previous dinner guidelines.
3. Involve all members of the family in deciding what they would enjoy doing together.

Family Night Ideas

- Have a healthy pizza night and play a fun board game. I recommend keeping "technology" games to a minimum, as this may not be anything new or different for many children. You will want to focus on the activity being interactive and involving everyone.
- Take a bike ride, and stop in a lovely spot for a picnic.
- Arrange children's sport activities and a family picnic afterward.
- Have a movie night with popcorn (choose a movie that is aligned with your family values and discuss what each person enjoyed most in the movie).
- Read about a country or a culture together, and create dinners around that culture.

> daily aspiration   "Today I send all my family members love and good health.

58 siblings: good stress and bad stress

Research is plentiful about how twin siblings tend to react alike in certain situations. A McGill University study found that nontwin siblings, too, can react similarly with regard to stress. Since stress is contagious, efforts to cut down on events that cause high stress may have a positive effect on your siblings. Recognizing and respecting the differences among siblings can reduce stress, as can using your emotional intelligence to learn when and why your siblings feel high levels of stress. The goal is to use that emotional intelligence to proactively eliminate or minimize instigators of stress.

dear diva

"What can I do to get along better with one of my two siblings, especially during the holidays when everyone is together?"

secrets from the de-stress diva

You don't choose your siblings. Although during childhood you shared the same roof over your heads, the same food, and the same parents (or variations of each), you and your siblings grow up to be so different from one another. These differences can certainly cause adult bickering and, in many families, a sizable fissure in siblings' relationships. It really doesn't matter so much why you're bickering as it does that you can step back, listen, respect your differences, and avoid getting caught up in the drama or the defensive remarks made by the other person.

Journaling is an excellent way to express your ideas, feelings, and emotions safely and constructively, especially during the holidays. Since it is not always appropriate to confront your siblings every time you don't like something they say or do, you need to create a space where you can let your feelings out, look at how the interactions make you feel, and then decide how you want to proceed with the relationship. I want you to go over your journal writings and every time you have blamed a sibling for something, put a little 'b" at the beginning of the sentence. This will give you an idea whether you're taking the victim role in the relationship or the communication. When you take on a victim role, you will continue to feel the pain because the very nature of being a victim means that something is happening to you and you have no control over it. As a child, this may have been true. But now, as an adult, you do have options and you are empowered to make choices.

One more thing: don't forget to forgive your siblings and then remember to forgive yourself as well. I once heard a great comment: "Not forgiving someone hurts you more than the person you don't want to forgive."

To maintain a positive relationship with your sibling, think of something that your sibling enjoys doing only with you. Spend quality time over the phone or in person with each sibling to keep the ties and the bonds strong.

Acupressure

Take the thumb of one hand and press it into the palm of your other hand for five to ten seconds. Breathe in and think calm thoughts, then put pressure on your other palm for five to ten seconds as you breathe out.

Feet Grounding

Elizabeth Andes-Bell, a yoga trainer in New York City, suggests doing the following exercises after a conflict with someone. They can be done in any position regardless of your location.

1. Place your hand very lightly over your solar plexus (between your heart and your belly) to calm the negative energy in a conversation or the churning feeling that you get in your belly when you obsess.
2. Focus on your breathing. "Take some calm, deep breaths and really feel the contact that your hand is making on your belly. You can feel your palm and all five fingers make contact," Elizabeth says. This is also a way to ground yourself, when you feel your own hand on your belly. It brings you back into your body.

3. Bring your awareness to the four corners of each foot: the ball of the big toe, the ball of the baby toe, the outer heel corner, and the inner heel corner. Remember that there are four corners on the bottoms of your feet in addition to five toes on each foot.

4. Stand up straight, breathe, and get into your body to ground yourself.

> daily aspiration   "I see my sibling as another human being with strengths and weaknesses."

59 surviving teenagers

Humans are becoming sexually mature before they are psychologically equipped to function as adults in society, researchers wrote in the journal *Trends in Endocrinology and Metabolism*. According to the study, "All our social systems work on the presumption that the two types of maturity coincide. But this is no longer the case and never will be again because we cannot change biological reality. We have to work out a new set of structures to deal with this reality."

dear diva

"I'm not ready for the emotional swings and the physical changes my children are going through. Is this puberty? How can I help my children through puberty to become a well-balanced, healthy, happy adults?"

secrets from the de-stress diva

Puberty is the period of human development during which physical growth and sexual maturation occur. Children in the United States and other developed countries are approaching puberty at younger and younger ages.

1. **Brace yourself with knowledge.** Your best weapon against puberty is knowledge. Once you recognize the physical changes involved, you will dramatically downshift your stress levels by understanding why your children are behaving in ways that are quite common with the onset of puberty.

2. **Don't avoid the S word, especially now.** Scientists say that today's children do not get the support they need from parents or society. Families and society in general should acknowledge the fact that some children are now biologically, sexually mature. As a parent or a friend, you must become more open about discussing sex with your children. Your physician or public librarian can recommend numerous well-written books for you and your children that can encourage frank discussions.

3. **Listen.** Every child approaches puberty at a different age and with a different attitude. It can be a very scary transition, especially for younger children. Create an environment that encourages your child to be open; then, listen. By listening carefully, you can assist your child through this often awkward period. This will also strengthen the parent-child relationship in a way that will prove less stressful and ultimately more rewarding throughout your lives.

4. **Take a social stand.** The controversies over sex education in public school are not at all in tune with the biological fact that children are sexually maturing at younger and younger ages. Children spend more hours each day in school and with their peers than with their parents. Children are more susceptible to peer pressure than adults are. Thus, as adults, we can strive to create a peer environment that is more knowledgeable about puberty. It's not about encouraging children to have sex; it's about equipping our children physically, emotionally, socially, and psychologically with knowledge about a very basic human function.

Eating Healthy Foods

Don't forget to introduce a wide variety of healthy fruits and veggies to your children and teenagers at the dinner table. Children will eat what's in the refrigerator. If you want your children to "nosh" on healthy foods, make extra helpings of lunches and dinners so that they have ready-made healthy snacks.

Role-Modeling

Children learn by what they see, not so much by what they're told to do. It is a parent's responsibility to learn the right way to act and then live it. If your anger is out of control, then learn how to control it; if you're sad a lot of the time or live with a high level of stress, learn how to get balance back into your life. There is no better way to teach children than by example.

Stress

If you notice your adolescent feeling stressed out, help him or her identify where the stress is coming from *and* how to reduce it, particularly through different types of activity and the reframing of thoughts.

> daily aspiration   "I teach by example."

60 parents: they know your trigger points

Coping with aging parents is becoming a major issue for baby boomers, especially for the "sandwich generation," those still caring for their own children. A 2007 poll by *USA Today*, ABC News, and Gallup of boomers who have living parents reported that 31 percent of them are providing personal or financial help to their parents. Nearly half say that it has caused them to suffer stress. People are living longer, which will exacerbate the challenges for boomers and, ultimately, for the children of aging boomers. Most boomers, after all, are in their fifties and early sixties.

Caring for an aging parent can create guilt (Am I doing enough?), anxiety (Are they okay when I'm not here?), anger (Why do they take up so much time or energy?), and depression, as people watch their parents' health deteriorate. The rapidly rising costs of nursing

homes, in-home health care, and medicines in the only industrial-
ized nation without national health care only serve to compound
the problem. Acknowledge the difficulty of caring for aging parents, and empower yourself with information about how to save
time and avoid emotional pitfalls. Here are some smart first steps
toward reducing your stress while you care for aging parents.

dear diva

"How do I have a good relationship with my parents when they
tend to be so critical of what I'm doing most of the time?"

secrets from the de-stress diva

Chances are very good that your parents did the best they could with
their limited experiences, expertise, and knowledge. This concept is
easier to understand once you become a parent. You realize as a parent that your baby does not come with instructions. Many times, you
practice parenting the way you were parented, or you go to the other
extreme and act completely opposite from your parents to avoid
repeating your father's or mother's poor parenting habits.

Exchange Positions

I would like you to try this exercise. Imagine yourself in your
parents' position when you were growing up, and remember the
stories and the stressful events they have shared with you over
the years. It is amazing what happens to your heart when you
can, just for a moment, try to put yourself in another's person's
shoes, no matter how uncomfortable they feel. What are the top
two things most parents really want for their children?

Aromatherapy

To bring clarity to a situation, Terri Hicks, a master aromatherapist,
suggests that you choose a favorite essential oil and make a mist to
spray in a room, to create a calm atmosphere. You can use:

5 drops basil essential oil
5 drops lemon essential oil
2 ounces distilled water

Combine these in a mist bottle and shake. Mist the room and the bed linens.

Focus Your Attention on What You Want

Life coach Elfreda Petorius said that whatever you give your attention to always gets bigger. So, if you are having problems with your parents and you perceive that they are not validating or supporting you with one of your choices, you have the power to change your anxious or hurtful feelings about this issue. If you focus on the hurtful and negative feelings, you only increase their prominence, according to Elfreda. Rather than let parental hot buttons bring you down, look at these for what they are: emotional triggers, not reality.

Yoga

Yoga isn't the solution to relationship stress, but it does provide a reservoir of emotional equilibrium and balance that helps when situations become tense. Yoga poses and stretches will reduce tension and get you back to your center, or a state of calmness.

1. Do a slow stretch in the area of your body that is affected by your mental state or thoughts.
2. If you feel slighted or neglected by your parents, stretch your back by arching it slowly and then doing this in reverse.
3. Roll your shoulders forward three times and backward three times.
4. Remember to focus on your breathing throughout the exercise.

> daily aspiration   "I accept my parents for who they are."

61 significant others and love relationships

Strong personal relationships have a direct impact on lowering stress. A University of Chicago study found that people who described themselves as lonely had a higher level of cortisol, the stress hormone that wreaks havoc on our bodies. Research also shows that people who describe themselves as involved in personal relationships with loved ones, friends, family, or others are more likely to experience a better quality of sleep, thus avoiding the stress that comes from inadequate rest. Yet relationships can also be a major source of stress when one person's stress is sensed and then felt by the other, when communications break down, or when a relationship with a significant other takes a back seat to work, children, or other factors. You can use proactive strategies to sustain loving relationships with significant others; this is more productive than ignoring high-stress warnings that can eventually destroy relationships.

What value do you place on your love relationships? If this is one of your top three values, does the time you spend on these relationships reflect your value commitment? Look at your calendar and count the hours per week that you spend quality time on your relationships with loved ones.

dear diva

"How can I find more time to spend with my loved ones?"

secrets from the de-stress diva

Love relationships: "Can't live with 'em . . . can't live without 'em." How many times have you heard those words muttered in jest or exasperation?

Loving relationships demand nurturing to thrive, yet too many of my clients find themselves complaining that they just don't have enough hours in the day for the demands of work and home, as well as time to enjoy and nurture relationships. Here are tips to help you acknowledge, nurture, and celebrate loving relationships with significant others and with everyone whom you love, without experiencing stress.

- **Revisit your priorities.** If you were forced to live without your significant other (or your children or your friends) for the rest of your life or without the particular job you have at this moment, which would you choose? Mentally acknowledge and visualize your priorities—write them down on paper—as a first step toward placing more value on your top priorities. This exercise will inspire and energize you to make more time for your loved ones.

- **Create "date nights" with your significant other.** Notice how you mentally and emotionally adjust to the schedule of Monday morning meetings at work or important holidays. Formally create a "date night" once a week for you and your significant other. Once date night becomes a part of your weekly routine, your desire to spend more time with a loved one will automatically be fulfilled. Just as emergencies sometimes force you to reschedule an important meeting at work, accept that you sometimes will have to reschedule (but not eliminate) your weekly date night.

- **Set up "play dates" with other loved ones.** Just as you schedule work meetings, make time for holidays, or have weekly date nights with your significant other, plan "play dates" with your children, friends, parents, or other loved ones. *Play* is the operative word because this term will reinforce that you want to have fun with your loved ones, not fulfill an obligation. For instance, imagine the positive reaction of your adult friends if you ask whether you can arrange a regular play date with them because you want to have more fun with them. Wouldn't you enjoy being asked, too?

- **Celebrate loving relationships.** Celebrating loving relationships does not require expensive gifts or trips. Slip a note into the briefcase or the lunch bag of your significant other, expressing your gratitude at being in a loving relationship. Send a "Just Because" card to a friend or a family member. Celebrate with hugs and laughter; both are free and are also invaluable in nurturing loving relationships.

Massage

The physical toll of high stress levels is the enemy of intimacy. Practice the art of gentle massage on your significant other to dissolve stress and make room for intimacy. Massage is a marvelous skill to learn and share. You can find a book on massage basics in bookstores or at your public library. Visit www.massage therapy101.com for tips on stress-reduction massages and sensual massage techniques.

Communicate with Your Hands

Just as you use the universal signal for "Check, please," when you are in a crowded restaurant or a café in another country where you don't know the language, you can use your hands to signal your care and concern for others. When you feel hurt, you can touch your heart as you express your hurt feelings or when you desire to apologize for hurting the feelings of others. Crossing your arms (and hiding your hands in the process) during a conversation can be perceived as a signal that you are closing yourself off to others; uncross your arms to signal that you are open to what others are saying. Be consciously aware of using your hands to express empathy and affection.

Identify Your Love Languages

Author Gary Chapman identifies five emotional love languages in his book *The Five Love Languages*. They are:

1. Quality time
2. Words of affirmation
3. Gifts
4. Acts of service
5. Physical touch

The crucial element here is to identify your most important love language and have your lover identify his or hers. Then, it is essential for you to "speak" in the other person's love language if you want your lover to understand you and feel loved by you.

---

daily aspiration   "I have a loving relationship with my significant
other and with my children and good friends."

62 everyone needs a friend

Here's how important friendships are to successfully reducing your stress: an often-quoted study from the University of California at Los Angeles (UCLA) reports a direct link between spending time with friends and experiencing a drop in stress. This is especially true for women, the scientists reported. When women gather together, estrogen triggers a calming response, while testosterone reduces the calming effect. A study from Harvard Medical School also found that the more friends a woman has, the less likely she is to develop physical impairments as she ages and the more likely she is to be happy. The goal is never to let friendships take a back seat to stressful situations in your life because having friends is a powerful weapon against that stress.

What top five qualities do you appreciate most in a friend? Now, look at your existing friends and see which ones match up to the qualities on your list.

dear diva

"I feel an imbalance in my friendships. I find that I do most of the calling and checking in. How do I get my friends to take the lead?"

secrets from the de-stress diva

I am lucky to have retained a strong relationship with one of my childhood friends since seventh grade. We parted ways during college and afterward because our life paths took us in different directions. I occasionally got a "hello" from her, but that was it. I would say that our friendship has become strong again in the last ten years.

Friendships are very important to your health, as studies continue to show, but only if those friendships foster good feelings. Unlike a bad relationship with a family member, where you simply *must* work on achieving peace and harmony with each other, with a friend you have the option of ending the relationship. If you find that your friendships are draining your energy or you feel bad after talking or being around certain friends, then you need to make some decisions. Here are a few ways to handle a friendship that is creating stress for you:

1. **Communicate respect and honesty.** Any good relationship depends on a strong level of respect and honesty. Communication is the best vehicle to extend this type of conduct. You and your friend may have some unconscious jealousies or miscommunications that were never discussed or taken care of. You may think that it's faster and easier to brush ill feelings under the rug, but those hurt or negative feelings only pick up more steam the longer they are not attended to.

2. **Reality of the friendship.** Perhaps your friendship has run its course. I read a wonderful poem that helps to put life and relationships in perspective. It validated my thought that not every relationship can withstand the test of time.

3. **Speak directly.** Try not to second-guess or jump to any conclusions until you have had an opportunity to talk to the person about the issue that's bothering you. Even though you may be very close and may share "everything" with each other, you would be amazed at how many things friends don't tell one another because they feel guilt or shame about their own family dynamics.

Toss Out the Word *Should*

The word *should* gives you and others the impression that they need to do something a certain way . . . and your way is the best. Friends and people close to you don't want to be told what to do. It takes its toll after a while. The word *should* also creates a form of pressure when you use the word for yourself or with your friends. Instead, use phrases such as "Have you thought about . . . ?" or "Would you like to hear another view?" or "Is this something you want to do or feel that you must do?"

Toss Out *Have To*

The way you use your words has a cumulative effect on your relationships. You may not realize their impact and in fact, the other person may not be aware of how your words affect him or

her, but over the long haul, these little nuances may have gar-
nered enough steam to finally burst one day. Saying "I have to"
or "you have to" implies that you don't have the power to make
a choice or that your friend must do what you say because you
now have taken control of that person's ideas, feelings, or actions.
You may want to replace "have to" with "choose to."

I remember when this slight change of wording made a big
impact on me. I was in the gym exercising, and a friend whom
I hadn't seen for weeks came into the gym. I thought that this
was strange because he was an avid gym goer. He said that he'd
hurt his leg and couldn't work out. He said that he would never
again say, "I have to go to the gym," but rather, "I get to go to the
gym." That comment stuck with me, and I am applying it right
now. As I work on this book, I changed my thinking and my
words to say, "I am so appreciative that I am writing this book
for others and that Wiley is my publisher," rather than, "I have
to write my book . . . a deadline is looming," both of which are
correct, but the latter comment brings on stress.

What's Your De-Stress Language?

Renee Piane, whom I call the "Italian Yenta," is a well-known
dating and networking expert who once said, "You need to know
how your friends de-stress before you know how to help them
relax." Renee has a group of women friends that meets monthly
by phone for emotional support; they allow each person ten
minutes to "emote."

Two other ideas that Renee recommends as de-stress strategies
are:

1. Reserve a certain amount of time that you can give so that
   you'll be present to really listen and validate your friend's
   feelings.

2. Don't try to fix a friend's problem; just let your friend vent.
   You might say something like, "How can I help to support
   you?"

A Gift of Value

Don't you find that oftentimes you feel really good when you give someone else a gift?

Give a gift to a friend for no reason other than the fact that you value the person's friendship. Sometimes the only thing a friend needs is to feel that you care and value his or her friendship. It's a great way to diffuse and decrease stress in a friendship.

> daily aspiration   "I value my friends, and they are a loving support for me."

63 create your supportive swat team

Friends and family can provide you with the support systems you need to reduce the stress in your life and help you to pursue a more rewarding lifestyle.

Researchers at the University of Tokyo found that the mere presence of a supportive individual in the room can prevent stress-related chemicals such as cortisol from being released.

You can create your own SWAT team to be on hand for times when you experience extraordinary stress triggers. You can also become a member of a SWAT team for your friends, family, and coworkers. Support systems can be made up of family members, friends, and coworkers or can even consist of resources or peaceful places that you can go to de-stress—all of these can help to reduce stress levels. Be strategic in planning how you can reduce stress, and seek out people who are positive and supportive.

dear diva

"The worst part about feeling overwhelmed during so many days of the week is that I feel so alone. I wish I had more help. I wish I had more support from, well, anyone. How can I get the support I need?"

secrets from the de-stress diva

Just as police departments rely on specially trained SWAT (Special Weapons and Tactics) teams for major crises, you can form your own SWAT team to have in place for unexpected emergencies to minimize the often agonizing stress that accompanies true catastrophes. With your own SWAT team, you can literally be in two places at once by having a SWAT team member take your mother to a medical appointment when you are home ill or finish a task at work when you need to be absent because your child sick is at home.

A SWAT team can be in place to provide support for major crises such as divorce or a death in the family. A SWAT team can be called on to help you solve a financial problem, help you to move from one city to another, or help you to cope with a relative in trouble.

The goal is to create your SWAT team *in advance* to be ready for life's emergencies. Ask a friend or a colleague to be on your SWAT team, and promise to call on his or her services only in case of a real emergency, not for mundane challenges. People often respond positively when you tell them that you want them to be a member of your SWAT team because you admire their skills and can depend on them in an emergency. Be profuse with your gratitude beforehand and after emergencies. Be amenable to your SWAT team members when you, in turn, are asked to belong to their SWAT Teams. Instead of suffering anxiety and stress from thinking, What if? What if? you'll be in control and prepared, knowing that whatever life brings, you have a SWAT team available.

Enlist a Mentor

Sometimes good advice at the right time can prove to be a powerful weapon against the stress instigators in your day. People who enlist the support of a mentor have access to that weapon every day. Libraries and bookstores have shelves filled with books on successful business and political leaders who gave credit for their success to mentors who advised and counseled them along the way. Take this cue to find a mentor in your profession or a person whom you admire for achieving balance in his or her home, lifestyle, and work. Ask that person to become your mentor. Attending professional association meetings and inviting friends with similar interests is a good way to find a mentor.

Make Two Calls

When you need support, make it a point to contact two people with whom you can share what's on your mind. Let them know that you don't expect them to do anything other than lend a friendly ear. You will be amazed at how open others are to giving this type of support.

> daily aspiration   "I am not alone ... the universe supports me in all that I do."

64 helping the feline in your life relax

Veterinarians say that cats are like humans in feeling stressed because of changes in their environment. The introduction of a new human into a household can cause stress, as can the change in a cat's environment created by its owner taking a new job with new hours. A move into a new home can also cause stress that may make your cat act withdrawn, become aggressive, or refuse to use the litter box. Patience and empathy are de-stressing responses that cat owners can manifest to minimize stress in their pets.

dear diva

"I'm afraid my cat is becoming withdrawn (or hostile) because of a stressful situation that I can't minimize right now. How can I create a home environment that is not stressful to my cat or myself, especially when I'm away at work or traveling?"

secrets from the de-stress diva

Cats can become withdrawn or hostile when anything changes in their lives. For example, a cat's human caretaker may get a new job, which will necessitate the person's going to work and coming home at different hours. Or the family may move to a new home, or a new human (a spouse or a child) may join the household. Gradually introduce your cat to any change to minimize destructive stress. Leave it alone for a few extra minutes each morning or evening to let it get used to the change. Make introductions to new humans gradually, a few minutes at a time. Always be with your cat when new humans are present, to create a familiar comfort zone. Introduce it to a new home one room at a time, for a few minutes at a time. Be sure to fill your new home with cat toys and bedding that are already familiar to your cat. Moving to a new home is not the time to throw away items that your cat is accustomed to. Patience is key.

Here are some other tips from the Humane Society of the United States:

1. Take your cat to the vet for regular check-ups. This is the smartest way to address any early symptoms of stress with professionals.

2. Spay or neuter your pet. Your cat will be healthier and therefore less prone to stress.

3. Give your cat a nutritionally balanced diet to avoid the stress of ailments caused by a poor diet. Always provide your cat with access to fresh water.

4. Groom your cat often to give him or her personal attention and also to prevent hairballs, which are the result of too much self-grooming.

5. Minimize your stress by consulting a veterinarian about how to train your cat to refrain from bad behaviors, such as scratching furniture or jumping onto countertops.

6. Visit the "Pets for Life" section at the Humane Society's Web site at www.hsus.org/pets to learn more about how to train and care for your cat.

Immunizations

Immunization for your cat is important, although limiting the number of unnecessary injections is critical as well. Dr. Shawn Messonnier said, "Anytime you inject a foreign antigen, such as vaccine, into the body, you alter the immune system, potentially triggering a negative immune response. Excessive immunization exposes your pet to a higher number of antigens, increasing his or her risk of an adverse reaction. In some cases, an animal develops a chronic symptom, such as joint soreness, or a more serious condition, like systemic lupus, as a result of repeat vaccinations." These responses are referred to as "vaccinosis" by holistic veterinarians. Ask your vet to give your cat a titer test that will determine the concentration of antibodies in your cat's bloodstream and will further reveal how your animal may be immune to a certain disease.

A Fun-Filled Inside Environment

It is suggested that if you do keep your cat mostly indoors, you try to create a warm and fun environment with:

- multiple play toys
- organized exercises
- places to climb
- rooms with a view
- outside bird feeders
- fish tanks
- edible cat grass

Car Sickness

It is best to take short trips with your cat or other pet when it is young so that it can acclimate to traveling. As for adult pets, you may want to avoid feeding them for a few hours before you begin your trip, to minimize nausea.

If your pet does get car sick, ginger sometimes helps animals that have nausea from car sickness. Most animals can't tolerate raw ginger root, so try one or two ginger cookies or a 500mg (or less) capsule of ginger powder. Or look for car sickness products in local pet stores containing ginger as an ingredient. Give the ginger to your pet at least thirty minutes before your departure.

Plan Play Time

One of the most rewarding aspects of owning a cat is enjoying each other's company. Cats love to play, especially with you. What better way to bond and de-stress!

> daily aspiration   "I spend quality time with my cat."

65 dogs need love, too

Having a pet—any kind of pet—is good for your happiness, your health, and your efforts to downshift the stress in your life. One UCLA study found that dog owners require less medical care than patients without pets do. Another study showed that the simple act of petting an animal can reduce a human's blood pressure.

dear diva

"I feel as if I am being punished when I come home to my dog's destructive behavior, which only happens when I'm away. How can I help my dog feel less anxious when I go out?"

secrets from the de-stress diva

Dogs are social animals. Veterinarians report that separation anxiety can cause your dog to create havoc while you are away and to become too aggressively happy to show affection when the leader of its pack returns home. Leaving toys in the house to keep your pet company is one way to lessen separation anxiety. Veterinarians can prescribe special medications for extreme cases of stress.

How to minimize separation anxiety. If your dog tries to knock you down with affection when you come home or you find evidence of destructive behavior, your dog is probably suffering from the stress of separation anxiety. Patience and advance planning are essential to minimize the stress on your dog and yourself. The goal is to gradually introduce your dog to your absences by separating your dog from you (in another room or part of the house) for a few minutes at first, then a few more minutes, then thirty minutes, and then an hour. Once your dog can be left alone for two hours, you will be able in most cases to leave your dog alone for the day.

Stay calm yourself. Just as you don't want your dog to knock you over with affection when you return from a trip to work or from doing errands, veterinarians advise that *you* do not act overly happy when you leave or when you return. Treat departures and returns with subtlety. Do leave a favorite chew toy when you go or a radio turned on to a low volume level. Dogs are social animals that will welcome the company of familiar sounds or a favorite toy when you're away.

How to Ensure That Your Dog Has a Healthy Diet

Like humans, more pets are becoming obese, which can lead to diabetes (yes, even in dogs!), arthritis, and heart disease. Veterinarians at www.petsmart.com suggest that one way to learn whether your dog is overweight is to place the palm of your hand on the side of the dog's rib cage and press gently. If you can feel your dog's ribs with this gentle pressure, your dog is probably at or near the correct weight. If you have to push harder, your dog might be overweight. A trip to the veterinarian will confirm your suspicions.

The science of pet nutrition is more advanced than ever, and your veterinarian can recommend pet foods for overweight dogs. Good nutrition is just as important as exercise to your dog, so keep your dog away from excessive doggie snacks. A healthy dog is a less stressed-out friend.

When You Travel

You have to make the decision whether to board your pet or hire a pet sitter when you travel for long periods of time. Your job will be much easier if your dog is sociable around strangers. If not, consider hiring a pet sitter whom you can introduce to your dog at least once before your departure to allow your dog to make a new friend. Just as you would with a babysitter, check a pet sitter's references and résumé and conduct an interview (with questions you have prepared in advance) to learn whether the pet sitter is right for you and your dog. Make your trip away as stress-free for your dog as it will be for you.

Great Web Sites for Dog Lovers

Dozens of terrific Web sites exist for dog lovers, often with "ask an expert" features, as well as active forums that will allow you to discuss your dog's care with other dog lovers. Among my favorites are: www.dogwise.com, www.petconnection.com, and www.workingdog.com.

The Humane Society of the United States also has a highly informative Web site about dogs and other pets at www.hsus .org/pets/pet_care.

> daily aspiration   "I love spending time with my dog."

66 taking care of ailing pets

As our pets get older, they often experience the aches and pains associated with the degenerative joint disease arthritis. In fact, many of our human conditions occur in our pets. According to a 2003 report by the National Academies' National Research Council, 25 percent of dogs and cats in the Western world are obese, thus making them vulnerable to more disease.

A survey done by the American Animal Hospital Association showed that more than 30 percent of pet owners have used alternative therapies on their animals.

dear diva
"How can I help my dog with arthritis pain?"

secrets from the de-stress diva

A healthy diet is as important for your animal as it is for you. Create a wholesome diet, avoiding commercial foods with fillers and preservatives. Prevention is very important with arthritis because once the joints become deformed, the damage is done. The veterinarians I have spoken to say that acupuncture has yielded positive results in the treatment of arthritis.

Tellington Touch

This noninvasive procedure uses a method of massaging with circular touches and long connecting strokes from head to tail. The long strokes mimic the way a mother dog licks her puppies from head to tail. This type of massage also provides an excellent means of bonding for pets and owners.

Food

Greg Howie, DVM, recommends a diet that he learned about while he was taking a veterinary acupuncture course. "Many animals improve on this diet alone," he said.

Ingredients

2 cups brown rice	1 cup parsley
2 cups barley (pearls)	2 cups spinach
1 cup lentils	2 cups lamb or beef heart
2 cups carrots	2 garlic cloves
1 cup celery	8–12 cups water

Combine the ingredients in a large covered pot. Bring this to a boil and simmer it for 1 ½ hours. Stir it often and add water if needed. Feed this to the dog daily for a month until you see improvement. Later, you can vary the ingredients, such as changing the meats and rotating the vegetables. The diet also helps with weight loss and boosts energy.

Anti-Inflammatories

John Heinemann, PhD, the author of *Natural Pet Cures: Dog and Cat Care the Natural Way*, suggests giving your pets "mineral-rich anti-inflammatories like alfalfa and yucca. Add them in powdered form to food once a day (¼ teaspoon each for cats; 1 teaspoon for dogs)." These reduce the swelling of arthritis.

Common Ailments in Aging Pets

A good resource to help you investigate the ailments of aging pets is www.drfostersmith.com, which offers dozens of articles and fact sheets on birds, cats, dogs, fish, and other pets.

daily aspiration   "My pet is receiving a lot of TLC."

household chores and charm

⭐ 67 de-stress your home

Home is supposed to be your sanctuary, but often it is just one more cause of stress in your already over-stressed life. Homes become battlegrounds for dysfunctional family relationships, and the long hours you spend in school and at work rob you of the time to clean and tend to your home environment. How can you truly make your house into a home, even with a limited budget?

dear diva

"When I come home from a hard day at work, I think of my house as just another battlefield, with chores piled up and waiting. I can't seem to get my house in order, and the thought of it exhausts me. How can I make my home more inviting not only for company, but for myself?"

secrets from the de-stress diva

1. **Create your own comfort zone.** Choose your favorite room in the house, and declare it your comfort zone. Make this room your quiet place, containing a special chair or another comfortable piece of furniture. Add books you love, soft lighting, candles with your preferred scent, and other items that will relax you. This room, or even part of a room, will be your very own de-stress sanctuary.

2. **De-stress your lighting.** Poor lighting can cause eye strain and can make you feel anxious and fatigued. Lights that mimic bright sunshine are the best. Open your windows to let natural light stream in, and purchase full-spectrum lightbulbs for your kitchen, living room, and home office.

3. **Simplify.** In this high-stress, time-starved world, simplifying your home environment can eliminate stress instigators. Buy bins and boxes that simplify your storage, and organize your belongings where they can easily be put away. Vow to remove ten items from each room, an extra lamp, a handful of knick-knacks, extra pillows on your sofa, an appliance from your kitchen counter, or souvenirs

gathering dust on a cabinet shelf. You'll find your rooms easier to clean and more relaxing, too, because you have created more uncluttered space.

4. **Turn down the noise.** Too much noise makes people anxious, so buffer noise sources throughout your home. Turn off the television set when you have company. Replace jarring music with relaxing tunes while you prepare dinner or work in your home office. Create a no-noise zone in your kitchen or your living room for certain hours of the day. Ask that all phone calls be made or returned away from general areas. Set all phones on "mute" during meals.

5. **De-stress your demands.** No one keeps a perfect house, so why create more stress for yourself by demanding perfection as a housekeeper? People get messy, so their homes will get messy. Relax and forgive yourself; you'll be surprised at how much more comfortable your family and guests will feel. Strive to be relaxed and imperfect, instead of tense and irritable trying to be perfect.

De-Stress Scents for Your Home

A favorite trick in the real estate business is to bake cookies in the oven on Open House days to welcome potential home buyers with the delicious aroma of childhood. Relaxing scents can de-stress any home environment. Many consider herbal or woodsy fragrances more relaxing than floral ones. Others prefer cinnamon or vanilla scents to suggest the aroma of something wonderful being baked in the kitchen.

Scented oils and candles can be found in specialty stores, grocery chains, department stores, and pharmacies. When you shop, buy whatever makes you feel most relaxed. Think light versus overpowering. Think calming versus invigorating. Share your shopping trip with others who live in your home to find a fragrance that will appeal to everyone. You can also scent bookmarks, pillows, and linens with clean, light fragrances to create a sense of relaxation and calmness in your home environment.

Aromatherapy

The hypothalamus is part of your limbic system, where your sense of smell and various stress responses are processed. This part of the brain helps you to relax when you smell certain fragrances. Relaxing aromas produce calming brain waves, such as delta and theta waves.

Some relaxing fragrances include lavender, bergamot, marjoram, sandalwood, lemon, chamomile, and valerian.

daily aspiration   "I have found the perfect spot to relax at home."

68 tackling room clutter

Much of your home clutter can be directly related to your mind clutter. Many of you are so busy doing what needs to be done that you rarely have the added energy to straighten up, put papers and clothes away, or perform other "small" chores. These minor tasks add up, however, and within a day or two, you have clutter.

Meditation is an excellent place to begin to keep clutter at bay. "Meditation helps your mind be healthier," explains Victoria Maizes, MD, the executive director of the University of Arizona's Program in Integrative Medicine. "That, in turn, helps your body respond better to challenges, no matter what you encounter."

dear diva

"Everyone just leaves their books, homework, papers, and other stuff lying around for me to pick up, and as a result, the house is full of clutter. The clutter makes me nervous, but I don't have time to clean it up. How can I keep my home de-cluttered without spending too much time or energy on it?"

secrets from the de-stress diva

The difference between making the task of de-cluttering your home a welcome activity or one of drudgery comes down to your intention and your thoughts during the process of cleaning up. While de-cluttering each room:

• Think of making space for something new to enter.

• Focus on cleaning up the stagnant energy in the room and creating good fortune.

• Visualize the new experiences, events, people, and opportunities you will bring into each room:

• Toss any item that doesn't celebrate who you are or doesn't serve a utilitarian purpose.

Aromatherapy

Choose your favorite essential oil and make a room mist to create calmness in a room. Suggested oils that benefit the nervous system and the mind include pine, peppermint, bergamot, bois de rose, geranium, lavender, lemon, vetiver, and ylang-ylang. Try mixing two or three of these oils together, combining a total of 12 drops with 1 ounce of carrier oil, to create your own personal favorite.

Use these oils to energize or bring clarity to a situation: basil, peppermint, rosemary, lemon, or grapefruit.

12 drops oil (any combination of the oils mentioned above)
2 ounces distilled water

Put these ingredients in a mist bottle and shake. Mist a room, bed linens, and outer clothing (such as school jackets).

Do One Thing at a Time

Plan to put away only one item every morning and one item every evening. Before you know it, you will feel confident that the room will be straightened up. You may even find the time and the energy to do thirty minutes at a stretch.

Do You Have Five Minutes?

Schedule a time and start to clear things away for only five minutes. You can make this a family event and get everyone involved for only five minutes. When the five minutes are up, announce loudly, "Five minutes." This may make it more fun for the children.

> daily aspiration
> "I am enjoying a peaceful, clean room."

69 housecleaning

We spend more hours at work and in school than any other generation has, leaving us less time for housework and leisure activities. If you value leisure time over housework, then de-stressing household chores should become your priority, in order to downshift your home life.

dear diva

"By the time I get home from work, I'm too exhausted to start cleaning. How can I get my house clean without spending hours each day on it?"

secrets from the de-stress diva

1. **Delegate.** Don't take on all of the housecleaning chores by your-self. Delegate weekly chores with a chart that you make, listing the person responsible, the day of the week, the chore, and the reward. Adding a column for rewards is important to motivate you and your family to succeed. If you live alone, delegate at least one day a month to inviting a friend or a relative to help you, or to hir-ing a one-day cleaning service to give yourself a welcome break. Budget by determining which restaurant outing or entertainment expense is worth skipping to bring in a cleaning service at least once a month.

2. **Spot clean each day.** Get a bucket and fill it with water and a clean-ing liquid. Take along a rag, paper towels, and a scrub brush with you when you shower in the morning to spot clean (quick clean) as you go. Ditto with every room you visit each day. Spot cleaning daily lets you avoid spending hours each week cleaning leftover messes.

3. **Choose a "clean sweep" day.** On "clean sweep" day, whether it's once a week or once a month, take your cleaning bucket from room to room and scour up. You can choose one room or two rooms per "clean sweep" day. Mark these days on your calendar to stay ahead of your mess.

4. **Don't be a maid to your things.** If you have too much stuff to clean, get rid of some of it. If you want to donate it, immediately put a box full of items to be given away inside your car trunk so that the box doesn't become one more thing to step over when you walk into your house.

5. **Integrate.** Incorporate pleasant or distracting activities into your housecleaning. While you fold clothes, watch a favorite show. Play dance music on your iPod or on the radio to energize yourself and exercise as you clean (and dance!) from room to room. Invite your children to describe their day while you clean the kitchen, and invite them to talk *and* help as you work.

6. **Forgive yourself.** Relax because there's no law against having a messy house. If you are stressed out, forgive yourself for neglecting the chore of housecleaning. The mess will still be there tomorrow, but you'll be in a better, calmer mood to attack it. If you get a surprise visit, laugh out loud about it. Laughter is contagious, and knowing that not everyone is perfect (nor are people's houses) is a refreshing break from the demands you place on yourself and others.

Baking Soda for Everyday Cleaning

Instead of using cleaning agents with toxic chemicals, switch to baking soda as an inexpensive and environmentally friendly cleanser for your house. Here are just a few of the dozens of ways you can make housecleaning easier with baking soda:

- Keep your bathroom and kitchen drains from clogging by pouring a half-cup of baking soda down the drain once a week.

- Cover the bottoms of pans that have stuck-on grease and grime with a layer of baking soda, add water, and soak them overnight. They're easy to clean up the next morning.

- Remove stains from floors and counters with baking soda and a sponge. Rub it in, let it sit for a few minutes, and wipe it away. Repeat for tougher stains.

- Fill a bucket with water and a handful of baking soda and clean your refrigerator and microwave with this. Your appliances will smell fresher, too. Leave an unopened box of baking soda on a back shelf of your refrigerator and freezer to keep them smelling fresh. Replace the box every two weeks or every month.
- Boost the power of your laundry detergent, or your laundry detergent plus bleach, by adding a half-cup of baking soda to the load.

Positive Energy in Your Home

Wherever activity frequently occurs in a house, such as in hallways or on the stairs, these circulation routes can be considered the meridians or the vital energy (chi) in a home. Keep these energy areas free of clutter.

> daily aspiration   "I keep up my housecleaning with ease."

70 laundry

Before the Industrial Revolution, most clothes were cleaned with steam or rubbed against rocks and rinsed in streams, which made doing laundry an environmentally correct but time-consuming chore. Today, most homes are conveniently equipped with washing machines and dryers or are located close to laundromats, which would cut down on the amount of time it takes to do laundry except for the fact that Americans own more clothes than in previous generations.

dear diva

"Laundry piles up when it's dirty, and it piles up when it's clean, waiting to be ironed or folded and put away. I can't seem to stay on top of it. How can I become more efficient at doing my laundry?"

secrets from the de-stress diva

1. **Set one day aside each week as laundry day.** Unless you have twelve children, doing laundry every day or even every three days makes it a chore. If you can focus your energy on doing laundry only one day each week, this will also allow you to schedule a time to sort, fold, iron, and put away your laundry afterward.

2. **Use your washing machine as your laundry bin.** Make it a habit to toss warm-water washable items into your washing machine basket throughout the week. On laundry day, your first load will be ready to go.

3. **Know the difference between "dry clean" and "dry clean only."** Dry cleaning is getting more expensive every year, so try hand-washing your "dry clean" (not "dry clean only") items with mild soap and cold water, and hang them to dry.

4. **Be kind to the planet.** Wash your clothes on the "cold" setting whenever possible. It's kinder to the planet by conserving energy and can also save more than $100 on your gas or electric bill each year. Use biodegradable soaps and dryer sheets, too.

5. **Integrate.** On laundry day, integrate a rewarding activity into this chore. Time your exercise routine by the number of minutes it takes to wash your clothes (aerobics) and dry your clothes (yoga, stretching, and cool-down exercises). Tell your children and spouse to save their favorite stories from the week for laundry day to share while you wash, fold, and put away clothes as a family activity.

6. **Delegate.** Assign each family member a laundry-based chore. One person will wash and dry, another can fold, and someone else can collect and sort dirty clothes.

7. **Throw away.** There will be less laundry to stress your day if there is less laundry to do. Give away clothes that you don't need, and reward yourself by promising yourself one new item of clothing for every five (or ten) items you give away. Just because clothes are relatively cheap does not mean that your time to clean, sort, and store them is cheap.

Getting Out Those Stains

Here are some stain-removing tips from www.about.com.

- To remove protein-based stains (blood, milk, body soils, eggs, baby formula), clean off the stain with a spoon before treating the fabric. Heat sets stains, so use cool water for washing and rinsing. Repeat, and repeat again, if it's an old protein-based stain. You will need to add liquid laundry detergent with enzymes (most laundry detergents fall into this category). You can also add an oxygen-based color-safe bleach product, which is great for removing standard stains.

- To remove dye-based stains (fruit, grass, mustard, juices), soak the stained area repeatedly. Unlike the instructions for protein-based stains, use hot, hot water and liquid detergent on dye-based stains.

- To remove tannin-based stains (coffee, colas, wine, tea), run the stained area under cold water (or wash it first with cold club soda) and then wash it with the hottest water possible. Use a liquid detergent in the wash. Stay away from bar soaps on your tannin-based stains because bar soap sets these stains. The tougher the stain, the more time you will have to spend repeating the stain-removing steps.

- To remove deodorant stains in the armpits of washable shirts, soak the stain in white vinegar, wait thirty minutes, and then launder with liquid detergent.

How to Keep Dark Clothes Dark

When washing dark clothes for the first time, use cold water and put a handful of salt in the water. The salt helps set the color. To brighten dark clothes after they have been washed several times and are starting to fade, repeat the procedure. To re-darken black clothes that already look brown after repeated washings, add coffee or strong tea to the rinse water. Always wash clothes inside out to keep them from fading.

daily aspiration   "I relax while doing my laundry."

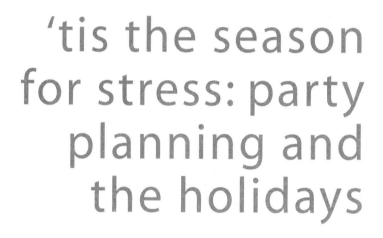

'tis the season
for stress: party
planning and
the holidays

71 seasonal changes

I love the four seasons. In Santa Monica, California, where I live, I experience only two: spring with a little rain and a few cold nights, and summer. Still, I can anticipate and celebrate all four seasons inside my head and in my home by visiting stores that promote the look and the scents of each season, by decorating my home a special way for each season, and by allowing myself to celebrate the positives of each season. There are many people, however, who find certain seasons sad. Seasonal affective disorder, called SAD, is a type of depression that follows the seasons. The most common type of SAD is called winter depression. It usually begins in late fall or early winter and goes away by summer. A less common type of SAD, known as summer depression, usually begins in the late spring or the early summer. It goes away by winter. Scientific studies have linked SAD to changes in the amount of daylight during different seasons. According to the American Academy of Family Physicians, as many as half a million people in the United States may suffer from winter depression. Another 20 percent might experience a mild version of SAD. SAD is more common in women than in men and occurs more frequently in northern geographic regions. Studies suggest that the incidence of SAD can decrease as people age.

Fall is also a time when many people realize that there are only twelve weeks left until the end of the year, and they become stressed at the overwhelming amount of work they must do before then. Or they feel stressed when anticipating the holiday responsibilities ahead.

Every season has its own pressures and to-do lists.

dear diva

"There's so much on my plate already, and now I need to adjust to all of the changes to my schedule, as well as more responsibilities that come with each season. How can I embrace each season and work with it, instead of running head on against it?"

secrets from the de-stress diva

Every season has its own stressors, especially if you have a family. First, let go of all of your previously stressful thoughts and feelings about holidays, end-of-the-school-year activities, summer planning for vacations, and child care. Instead, create opportunities for each season.

DE-STRESS FALL

The start of fall means there are twelve weeks left until the end of the year. Instead of feeling panicked, make this your opportunity to create a positive game plan for how you will reduce your stress in time for the holidays. Plan ahead for the holidays in a way that will allow you to better accommodate or avoid altogether the stressful aspects of the holidays. Get ready for a better new year by beginning now to throw out old things, erase negative thoughts, and set mini-goals that you can celebrate every time you achieve one. Identify a fun activity that is related to this season, and enjoy it with family or friends.

DE-STRESS WINTER

What a beautiful time of year to savor nature's gifts: snow, "toasty" evenings around the fireplace. Invite your friends and family to feast on holiday comfort foods from your childhood. Enjoy special vegetables of the season. Identify one pleasurable activity that you will commit to doing this season, and have fun. Simplify your life and eliminate stress by reducing the size or the number of holiday events in your schedule. Then relax and really savor the holidays.

DE-STRESS SPRING

Again, what a beautiful time of year! You have more time to do things outdoors because of the time change that creates additional hours of daylight. Enjoy a favorite spring activity. This is your opportunity to celebrate the outdoors by visiting a community festival, a street fair, or another special event. Search the Internet for the word *spring* and the name of your community to find a fun spring event to attend.

DE-STRESS SUMMER

Alas, you are no longer a child who can look forward to celebrating a three-month break from school. But you can celebrate mini summer vacations away from your job and home responsibilities. Create a calendar of mini summer vacations that can last a day or even just an hour. Pencil in a "play date" to enjoy with friends or learn an outdoor activity. Visit a farmers' market. Take the whole family to rummage sales, and give each person a dollar to find a funny item that will make others in your family laugh out loud. Spend a lunch hour with colleagues having a picnic outdoors or checking out the sample cases at a nearby store.

Using Light Therapy

Light therapy is a proven and inexpensive way to dispel SAD during the dark winter months. The goal is to allow sunlight to hit the back of your neck for about fifteen to twenty minutes each day, which can offset SAD symptoms and trigger your body's response to reset your biological clock. If there is no sunshine, use a powerful electric light.

Using the Lightbulb inside Your Head

Writer Nancy Christie, who created the Web site "Community of Change," has another definition for SAD: "seasonal achievement dissatisfaction." Like the clinical version of SAD, Christie's SAD surfaces in the latter part of the year with defeatist thinking in people who think it's too late to make a change or a new start. For this disorder, you won't need a full-spectrum lightbulb in your house. Christie says, "All that you'll need is the lightbulb you want to shine inside your head." Identify the reasons why you're unhappy with a particular season, which will allow you to make the necessary changes in your life to eliminate your inertia. Let your inner lightbulb cast a light on the future, instead of on the past.

Setting Up a "Laugh Factory"

It has been shown time and again that you can't be stressed and feel good at the same time. It has also been proved that laughter actually causes beneficial hormones to be released in your bloodstream and helps you to de-stress, however briefly. Sometimes, this is all that's necessary to give yourself a breather from feeling stressed. In addition, this gap in stress creates a break in the downward spiral of your obsessive thoughts, which are the cause of much of your stress.

Comedian Stephen Colbert lived through a tragic accident in his family when he was ten years old. His father was flying with two of his brothers to enroll them in a New England prep school when their commercial flight crashed. All three were killed. Colbert knows and understands fear. Here's what Colbert has to say: "Not living in fear is a great gift, because certainly these days we do it so much. And do you know what I like about comedy? You can't laugh and be afraid at the same time—of anything. If you're laughing, I defy you to be afraid."

- Rent or buy comedies that you find funny, and make it a point to watch at least twenty minutes of one in the morning (to pull yourself out of an emotional slump) or twenty minutes before bedtime (to stop the obsessive stress thoughts and relax yourself to sleep).
- Surround yourself with positive people; run from negative ones. Or, if you have a family member who is negative more than positive, perhaps you can watch the funny videos together.

Aromatherapy

Aromatherapy can help you to embrace each season. Think back to the smells that made you happiest when you were a child during a certain season. You can purchase hundreds of thousands of scented candles and oils in stores or online. Does the smell of cooking (vanilla, pumpkin) make you feel good in the fall? Does the scent of Christmas (pine, cinnamon) make you feel like smiling during the winter? Does spring mean the fragrance of spring flowers and summer the smell of the sea? Buy scented seasonal candles and oils "off season" when they are on sale, and set them aside in a special place to help you anticipate all that is good about the coming season.

daily aspiration   "I embrace each new season."

72 de-stress airports

In our post-9/11 world, airports have become an especially high instigator of stress, with even longer security lines and often intimidating (and intrusive) security inspections. A study by Silverjet at London's busy Heathrow Airport linked airport stress to unhealthy physical changes in people's bodies. The study found that passenger heart rates peaked to four times their resting levels and that physiological stress levels exceeded those of Formula 1 race car drivers. The bright lights and the loud noises have also been shown to increase blood pressure and cause other signs of stress, especially during long layovers at overbooked, overly busy U.S. airports.

dear diva

"All the jostling and the crowds make me feel ill at the thought of having to go to the airport, especially when so many flights end up being delayed. How do I survive this without being miserable? I don't want to give up travel. How can I survive traveling through airports without becoming stressed?"

secrets from the de-stress diva

1. **Be healthy.** Get plenty of sleep and eat healthy foods on the days before your trip. You want to be in top physical condition to survive the physical stress of waiting in long lines, being jammed into cramped seating on the plane, and coming into contact with crowds of people who are teeming with germs. Drink veggie juices and eat a lot of fruits and veggies with vitamin C.

2. **Be prepared.** When you pack, ask yourself whether you can survive a day or longer of delayed flights with what you have in your bag. Look at what you plan to wear. Are your shoes and clothing comfortable? Keep all medicines in your carry-on baggage.

3. **Stay healthy.** Once you arrive at the airport, make it a point to drink plenty of water at every opportunity to avoid the

dehydration that results from air travel. Bring a hand sanitizer with you to use everywhere to avoid germs. Avoid caffeine and heavy foods. Stretch and walk often, even on the plane, to avoid blood clots that might occur from your being seated for long periods.

4. **Avoid the noise.** Bring disposable earplugs to drown out loud noises from the airport and on the plane. On long flights, use a sleeping mask to soothe yourself into a restful nap.

5. **Be ready for delays.** Have all of your flight and contact information available, should your flight be delayed. If the flight is delayed, shortcut the long lines by using your cell phone to reschedule flights or book lodging. Have magazines, paperbacks, or puzzle books with you to distract yourself during the long waits.

6. **Breathe.** Practice deep breathing to calm yourself when you are standing in noisy lines or during takeoffs and landings. Breathe in deeply; breathe out slowly.

7. **Don't forget your sense of humor.** Stress is contagious, which can be disastrous for you and those around you during crowded flights or when flights are delayed in overbusy airports. Use your journal to record the humor in the situation, and you'll have an entertaining tale to tell when you arrive home or at your destination. If you still feel as if you want to cry, treat yourself to a funny book or magazine at the airport gift shop.

About Traveling with Electronic Devices

Now that security checkpoint crews are allowed to inspect your laptop, cell phone, and other electronic devices at will, protecting these expensive belongings can become another cause of stress at the airport. First, ask yourself whether it is essential that you bring along this equipment. Then, remember to charge your electronic devices before you leave home, in case the inspectors ask that you turn on your laptop or other gadgets for inspection. Pack cords and batteries in a separate compartment to avoid their becoming mixed up with other travelers' possessions at the security checkpoints. Or, consider using a package delivery service to ship your electronics to your destination ahead of your flight.

In-Flight Exercises

Ankle circles. Lift your foot off the floor and draw a circle in the air with your toes pointed, alternating directions. Continue for thirty seconds. Repeat with your other foot.

Foot pumps. While keeping your heels on the floor, point your toes up as high as possible toward your head. Put both feet back flat on the floor. While keeping the balls of your feet on the floor, lift both heels high. Continue pumping your feet forward and backward for thirty seconds.

Knee lifts. While seated, march slowly in place by contracting each thigh muscle and lifting each knee. Continue for thirty seconds.

Knee to chest. Grab your left knee and pull it up toward your chest. Hold it there for ten to fifteen seconds. Slowly return it to the floor. Alternate your legs, ten times each.

(Source: *American Way* in-flight magazine)

---

daily aspiration
"I have good experiences at the airport and while flying."

---

73 dinner parties

Some of the greatest causes of stress in life, generally, are also factors when you throw a dinner party: money, poor time-management skills, and impossible expectations. Holidays generate stress because you often spend too much money entertaining too many guests. Even during other times of the year, these same stress factors can ruin your good intentions if planning a dinner party leaves you feeling exhausted and financially strained. Yet you can avoid getting caught in this trap. It *is* possible to create an inviting environment for yourself and throw a great dinner party for your guests. Let's see how.

dear diva

"I love the idea of having dinner parties, but I'm so afraid they won't turn out well that I get stressed out before, during, and after these events. I end up not enjoying myself and worrying that my guests are not having fun, either. How can I host a great dinner party without going into stress overload?"

secrets from the de-stress diva

Socializing over a great meal can be a rewarding experience for the host and the guests. It's a recipe for success, unless stress makes it a disaster. Here are a few smart tips to help you give a wonderful dinner party that everyone can enjoy.

1. **Plan ahead.** Make a budget and stick to it, and you'll avoid the financial stress that you might feel when you spend too much to entertain guests. Plan your meal and the number of guests according to that budget. Think back to simple meals you've had with good friends that were just as enjoyable, if not more so, than lavish dinners. Create a budget, and plan your meal according to that budget, leaving a little "wiggle room" for unexpected guests or mistakes in the kitchen. Shopping ahead for bargains is the smart way to stay within your budget. Also, if you have a tight budget, limit your guest list. Three guests can have just as much fun as thirty.

2. **Know your audience.** Plan your event to meet the personalities and the needs of your guests. If your guests don't know one another, schedule a pre-meal time with cocktails and appetizers to give your guests an opportunity to meet one another. If you know that several of your guests tend to be late, invite them to be at your dinner thirty minutes earlier than the time you tell other guests to arrive. If small children or older guests are on your list, accommodate their dietary needs with simple foods.

3. **Stick with tried-and-true recipes.** Don't use dinner parties as opportunities to experiment on your guests. Be confident by serving a recipe that you know is a success. If you want to try a new dish, make it a week beforehand to give yourself time to adjust any of the ingredients to your taste. Long before you prepare your meal, invite a friend to help you choose dishes that complement one another.

4. **Keep it simple.** You can use a complex recipe but also keep it simple by using pre-made salads, breads, side dishes, or desserts to accompany the dish. Guests will appreciate a simple meal served by a relaxed host more than they will a complex meal served by a stressed, exhausted host. So keep everything simple, including the layout of your dinner table. If you find yourself becoming anxious about the possibility of someone breaking an expensive piece of china or crystal, then don't use those dishes

5. **Clean as you go.** Clean the pots and the pans as you prepare the dishes to eliminate the stress of knowing that a big mess awaits you after the dinner party. Prepare dishes a day in advance and freeze or refrigerate them to minimize the mess. Assign members of your family who can't cook to the cleaning detail.

6. **Be flexible.** Things can go wrong before or during even the most carefully planned dinner parties. Acknowledge this fact beforehand, and you'll be less stressed when a dish is dropped, guests arrive late, or two best friends argue at the dinner table. If you become upset at a disaster, your guests will sense your anxiety and it will ruin their dinner. Smile, and your guests will smile, too.

Setting the Mood for Yourself

Before you set the mood for your dinner party, set the mood for yourself as the host.

Staying up late the night before the dinner party cooking, baking, or setting the table is counterproductive to your emotional and physical well-being. Health practitioners say that going to bed before midnight, even one hour before midnight, is three times more valuable than going to sleep one hour after midnight. It's all about your natural biorhythms, so don't cheat yourself out of a restful night's sleep before your dinner party.

If you wake up feeling stressed, use antistress aromatherapy. Certain essential oils, such as peppermint, geranium, or orange, are stimulating and are wonderful stress busters that can energize your brain when you inhale deeply and exhale deeply.

The power of positive aspirations can go far toward reducing your stress. Before your dinner party, say this out loud (and visualize it as you say it): "Everyone at my dinner party is having fun, including me." Enliven the atmosphere while you plan the party by playing upbeat music.

74 children's parties

The traditional backyard children's party has today become a source of high stress, as the media and the affluent in our society transform these events into large, lavish, often catered affairs. Parents who want to keep up with the neighbors also feel the peer pressure experienced by their children, who don't want to be different from their friends with their gala parties. Often, we forget that the celebration is for children, not adults.

dear diva

"I want my child to have the same lavish parties that his friends at school do, but the expense and the noise and the work make me feel stressed at the thought of throwing a children's party. Help! How can I host a successful children's party without stressing myself or the children?"

secrets from the de-stress diva

1. **Set a budget, and stick to it.** In the party budget, include the cost of any presents you buy for your child, as well as the costs of the food, trinkets, and toys for each child. Spare yourself the financial stress of throwing a children's party long before you set the date. You can save money by choosing simple foods and making party favors yourself.

2. **Limit the guest list.** Having too many guests will rob your child of the attention you want to give him or her on this special occasion. Some parents set their children's guest lists by their children's age. For example, they will invite five children to their children's fifth

birthday. If your child insists that everyone in his or her class be invited to a party, and this number does not fit your budget, then don't invite any members of his or her class; instead, invite cousins or neighborhood children.

3. **Involve your child from the start.** Involve your child in planning his or her own party. Allow your child to contribute to choosing a theme, healthy (your emphasis!) foods, games, and party favors. Your child will be more eager to help you prepare for the party if he or she can have a say in planning it.

4. **Don't create stress for other parents.** Don't create financial stress for parents of guests by creating a situation where expensive gifts are expected. Instead, write a note on the invitation encouraging only small or even homemade gifts. Or ask that each guest bring a photograph to be included in a party scrapbook.

5. **Keep it simple.** Children are children, so don't create a party setting that invites spills, breaks, and other messes. Keeping it simple will also make the postparty cleanup easier.

6. **Personalize party favors.** Take a picture of your child in a whimsical pose, and make copies to paste on low-cost toys, boxes, or other items. A Polaroid camera, in which photos are instantly developed, can provide a wonderful sense of fun. Children can take photographs of one another as keepsakes to take home. Or have each child create a funny drawing to share or for the scrapbook.

7. **Confine the mess.** If you are stressed beforehand at the mess a children's party will entail, choose a designated area of your home, a park, or your yard to confine the mess. Remove any breakables, and keep trash bins at the edges to toss as you go. Or, consider having the party off premises at a local pizza parlor.

8. **Stay flexible.** This is a children's party, which means there are more opportunities to break things, be noisy, and make messes. Accept that being noisy and making messes are fun for children, and incorporate "noisy zones" and "messy zones" into the party as your cheerful response to what you cannot control.

9. **Teach good manners.** Long before the party, teach your child to properly greet each guest and acknowledge any presents. Purchase or have your child make thank-you cards in advance to thank guests for attending or for gifts. Play "What if?" with your child. What if your friends get into a fight? What if someone

breaks something? What do you do when someone starts to cry? Discuss appropriate responses with your child before the party. It's the smart way to prepare your child to become a thoughtful adult.

Nature as Your Theme

Natural settings can reduce stress in children, according to a study by two Cornell University environmental psychologists. The researchers found that children who have access to natural settings suffer less stress than those who live and play in environments where there is no access to nature. To de-stress children's parties, consider a picnic in a natural setting such as a backyard, a park, or a trip to the zoo. If you don't have access to nature, consider a nature theme such as wild animals, zoo animals, trees, or forests and use enlarged photographs, information sheets, and toys and treats that have a nature theme.

Make Learning Fun

Incorporate learning experiences into your child's parties. Include notes about the history of items in a simple treasure hunt. Set up a make-your-own-dessert table with fruits cut into fun shapes to mix and match. Have a bulb-planting party, and prepare instructions so that each child who takes home a miniature pot will know when to expect the bulb to bloom.

daily aspiration   "The greatest gift I can give to my children is to love them."

75 cocktail parties

C ocktail parties can be a wonderful way to bring friends and acquaintances together for conversation, fun, food, and drinks. They can also be stressful occasions for hosts who do not carefully plan these social gatherings.

dear diva

"What if I can't pull it off, and I end up with a cocktail party full of disgruntled guests and embarrassing silences, instead of great food and fun? How can I be stress-free and also throw a relaxed, fun-filled cocktail party?"

secrets from the de-stress diva

1. **Set your time, date, and theme.** Most cocktail parties, on average, last two hours. Set the time and the date for your cocktail party, making sure that the date does not conflict with stressful occasions that are scheduled on days before or after the cocktail party. If you are anxious that guests will linger after the typical two-hour cocktail party, time it to bump up against another event, such as a cocktail party before a formal company dinner.

2. **Create your guest list.** Most cocktail party experts agree that ten to twelve is a good number of guests for an average cocktail party, although you can invite as many as twenty-five or more if your budget and personal comfort zone allow. Invite good friends, old friends, and casual acquaintances to allow guests the option of knowing some people at your event, as well as a chance to meet new friends. Keep in mind that cocktail parties are not for children, so discourage guests from bringing them. If all of your guests have small children, perhaps you can arrange a separate children's party at a friend's home at the same time.

3. **Create your invitations.** Create e-mail (casual) or handwritten (more formal) invitations that include the date, the time, the theme, and the dress. Example: Join us for a cocktail party featuring fine regional wines and exotic foods from 6 P.M. to 8 P.M. on December 15 at (address). Dress: cocktail dresses and suits. Another

example: Join us for a cocktail party celebrating martinis, cool food, and smooth music from 6 P.M. to 8 P.M. on November 3. Dress: casual. Encourage guests to RSVP, which will allow you to better plan the right quantities of foods and drinks to have on hand.

4. **Create a menu that matches your theme.** Plates of various appetizers are the best way to feed your guests at a cocktail party. Plan your foods to match your theme. For a holiday party, decorate your room and foods in holiday style. For a martini party, create some appetizers that are served chilled in martini glasses. Make the ingredients fit your budget. Do a Web search for cocktail party appetizers, or check out a book on appetizers to find hundreds of recipe ideas that fit any budget.

5. **Mix and match your foods.** Serve simple appetizers next to appetizers with complex ingredients to provide your guests with the widest choice to suit their palates. The advantage of appetizers is that you can serve many different kinds.

6. **Hire help.** Consider hiring a bartender, if your budget allows it, or ask a good friend to be your amateur bartender. This will free up your time to play host instead of server.

7. **Create a hospitable environment.** Clear all breakable objects and clutter from the room where you will entertain. Place chairs (and small tables if you have them) in locations that encourage guests to sit and talk comfortably and that create easy-to-navigate passageways. Folding chairs are fine for cocktail parties because guests can easily move them around the room.

8. **Stock plenty of ice and glasses.** Stock more ice than you think you'll need, and have two glasses on hand for each guest to ensure that no one has to wait while you wash out a glass for him or her to be served a different drink.

9. **Decorate according to your theme.** Decorate informally and use inexpensive plates and glasses for casual cocktail parties. Bring out the linens and the good plates for formal parties. Fresh flowers are a welcome addition to either casual or formal cocktail parties.

10. **Introduce every guest.** As host, you are responsible for introducing each guest to every other guest. As a conversation starter, add an interesting fact about your guests when you make your introduction. Example: "John, have you met Mary? Mary is the CEO of Company X and is also an avid basketball fan. John is an artist and also a wonderful cook who specializes in Italian foods."

11. **Let the dishes sit.** While you mingle, spend a few minutes gathering dirty plates and dishes and whisking them off to the kitchen (and ask a friend to help you in this chore), but let the dishes sit in the sink or on the kitchen counter. Devote all of your attention to your guests, and resolve not to clean up until after the party.

Stocking Up for a Cocktail Party

First, have plenty of nonalcoholic drinks on hand for people who don't imbibe. Second, have an exit plan for guests who don't want to drink and drive, with a list of taxi service telephone numbers available. Cocktail parties can be limited to wine or beer, can include a mix of liquors, or can have a combination of these.

How much should you buy for your cocktail party? According to the experts at www.fabulousfoods.com, a standard formula is to estimate that ten guests will consume twenty drinks at an average cocktail party and as many as forty drinks at a long cocktail party that usually also includes dinner.

A 750-milliliter bottle of alcohol will yield about sixteen cocktails; a liter bottle, twenty-two; and a 1.5-liter bottle, about thirty-nine drinks.

For a party of wine drinkers, five 750-milliliter bottles will yield about five drinks per bottle.

For beer drinkers, stock five six-packs for ten people, based on a 12-ounce serving. For more information about which liquors and mixers to stock, based on your budget, visit www.fabulous foods.com.

Fun Cocktail Party Recipes

Make your recipes fit your cocktail party theme. For example, you can find martini-theme cocktail food recipes at www.martiniart .com. For a French theme, go to www.frenchfood.about.com. For other ideas, visit Web sites such as www.thatsthespirit.com. Your public library also is a great resource for books that will provide you visual cues, as well as time-tested recipes.

daily aspiration   "My focus is to have fun and build memories."

76 holiday decorations

Holidays can be fun and can fill your home with warmth and love. The main idea is to keep the holidays simple and beautiful. I know so many people who do not entertain during the holiday season because they feel that their holiday decorations are inadequate or not as beautiful as those in someone else's home. The decorations don't matter as much as the warmth that you, your family, and your friends share while being together. Every day is set up to create new memories. You don't have to focus so much on the holidays for this to happen. In fact, when you become too stressed over making the holidays super special, you lose minutes, hours, and days that could be spent enjoying the simple pleasures of the season.

dear diva

"I really do love the holidays, but they take me over the edge with too many things that I need to do. How can I make the holidays more relaxing?"

secrets from the de-stress diva

Much of this holiday pressure is created because this is the time that children are home from school, members of your extended family come to visit, and friends want to share some holiday cheer with you. The biggest time pressure, however, is caused by your wanting to do too much. What would a relaxing holiday look like for you?

Here are some ways to create simple and beautiful holiday decorations.

ORANGE LIGHTS WITH PUMPKINS

1. String small orange lights on bare tree branches.
2. Insert the branches into pumpkins for support.
3. Set several of these outside and inside your home.

Variation: You can insert thick rosemary stems into pumpkins along with the lights.

Holiday Flowers and a Nature Hunt

Every Thanksgiving, for the last few years, I have gone on a nature hunt before Thanksgiving, where I pick up beautiful pine cones, leaves, and any other "fall droppings." I then take these precious pieces, add miniature fresh pumpkins, gourds, avocados, pears, pomegranates, and any other fruits or vegetables that we will eat within the next couple of days. I may place a few votive candles or miniature lights on the main table and around the house.

- Fill vases, urns, and window boxes with fall flowers such as mums, pansies, or decorative cabbages.
- Place a large fall leaf under a glass plate for a very effective and simple holiday place setting.
- Write the name of your guest on a fall leaf and place it under the glass plate.
- Attach past holiday cards to a wire, a string, or a cord with decorative clips and hang them over a mantel or a kitchen window or create a wall arrangement with them.
- Frame past holiday cards and put them on table tops. You can also use glitter, glue, or beads to update or embellish them or create a color theme.

What Is Your Collection?

Lee Ann Martin, the chef and the owner of the Country Rose Tea Room in Bakersfield, California, said, "Everyone has a collection of something." She urges everyone who wants to decorate for the holidays to ask themselves, "What do I have in my home?" Do I collect tea pots, tea cups, figurines, butterflies? You can make table decorations with your beautiful and treasured collectibles.

Celebrating Memories

The holidays are about celebrating memories, old and new. Take out family pictures that were tucked away, a special pitcher from Grandma, china and heirlooms that were in storage, and add the "old" yearly decorations to the mix as well.

daily aspiration   "My holiday decorations will be made up of memories stored in my home this year."

77 holiday entertaining

The holidays occur in a season when the weather usually changes, and there is a new energy and rhythm all around. It is a perfect time to take a moment and think of what you were doing a year ago and how much further along you are today. Holidays are also a time to create new traditions and memories. The hallmark of a holiday is to enjoy it from the inside out.

What are the top three things you value most in your holiday entertaining this year?

dear diva

"How do I entertain for the holidays without creating any more stress in my life?"

secrets from the de-stress diva

I celebrate a lot of holidays throughout the year because I love their cyclical nature, the special foods and spices for each one, the decorations around the house, their traditional meanings, and most important, the fact that they're an opportunity for every member of my family, or at least most of them, to reconnect and enjoy one another.

Here are a few tips that make it easier for me to cope during the holidays. They may work for you, too.

- Take a cup of tea, sit down in a quiet place, and think of the three most important things or feelings you would like to experience on this holiday.
- Plan in advance as much as you can what it will take to turn your vision from the previous idea into reality.
- Here is a checklist that I use (for a more in-depth list, please visit www.destressdiva.com/holidays).
  - Straighten up the front room, the kitchen, and any other area that people see when they walk into the house.
  - Bake or buy desserts and put them in the freezer at least a week in advance.

- Cook or buy cooked foods for the holiday and put them in the freezer at least a week in advance.
- Set the table and decorate the home and the table two to three weeks in advance, but don't set the festive tableware down until a day or two before the event. This is a great way to get into the mood of the holiday and enjoy the holiday longer.
- Make up a menu list for the day or the days of the event.
- As you invite your guests, share with them what they can bring to the party, the dinner, or the event. This will save you time and energy, instead of having to call them later to let them know.
- A week beforehand, plan what you'll wear each day of the event, just in case you have to do a wash, go to the cleaners, or pick up an extra top.

Serving Soup

Soup is a delicious and simple meal to serve when you are entertaining. Stack two or three cake stands and fill each tier with an assortment of fresh breads and rolls.

Make seasonal food decorations for your soup:

1. Slice a piece of cheese and use a seasonal cookie cutter to make the impression—a heart for Valentine's Day, a pumpkin for Halloween, and so on.
2. Place the variously shaped pieces of cheese on top of chili, soup, and so on.

Pumpkin Candles

1. Carve out a hole in each mini pumpkin that is the size of the bottom of the candles you're using.
2. Insert a candle into each mini pumpkin so that the candles fit well and don't fall down.
3. Place each pumpkin on top of a wide candlestick and light the candles. Voila!

A Time to Give

Each time you entertain and have guests visiting your home, ask them to bring pajamas, hats, gloves, or anything else warm that can be given away to those less fortunate. Keep a large basket in the entryway where everyone can place his or her gift to be donated. This new tradition will put most of your guests in the holiday spirit, and they may even start something similar at their events.

> daily aspiration
> "The holidays remind me to feel peaceful within and to be grateful for all that I have."

a note to my readers

I hope that by learning how to downshift the stress in your life, you will find more time and new opportunities to enjoy whatever is uplifting in your life.

As with anything important, learning how to de-stress your days takes time, practice, and patience. Be patient with yourself. This book was arranged to allow you to revisit pages that will become more relevant as you experience new challenges, new relationships, and new opportunities. Embrace what is positive and what inspires you.

Others will come into your life for a reason, for a season, or for a lifetime. I first heard those words from a friend, Jethro Singer, a professional photographer and a writer. I would like to share this poem that I wrote for all of you.

> May you go with abundance in health, wealth, and in everything you treasure . . . and know that when things don't work out the way you want them to . . . that somewhere there is a reason for the unreasonable and a light in all darkness. To remember that one lit candle can light up a dark room and that one lit candle does make a difference as long as the flame is burning. May you be that light within your family and among the world that makes the difference and burns brightly!

I applaud you, I support you, and I validate you for all your efforts—the big ones and the smaller ones. I learned a long time ago that it really isn't the size of the gift that is important—rather, it is the intention you place behind it.

I would love to hear from you. Please feel free to contact me at rklein@ruthklein.com, and you'll be able to find more de-stress tips at www.destressdiva.com. If you would like advice on ways to downshift, sign up for my free De-Stress Diva newsletter.

Now that you have read and picked up some de-stress tips, I have a gift for you. Just go to www.destressdiva.com/bk to receive it. I hope you like it!

Here's to you . . . with all of the beauty, power, and value that you bring to the world.

index